D1161412

AMERICAN
IMMIGRATION

Volume 1

The Story of American Immigration

GROLIER
EDUCATIONAL

First published in the United States in 1999 by Grolier Educational,
Sherman Turnpike, Danbury, CT 06816

When referencing this publication, use the following citation:
American Immigration. 10 volumes. Danbury, CT: Grolier Educational, 1999.

Photo Credits:
Pages 1, 3, 4, 5, 7, 9, 11, 27, 30, 31, 33, 42, 45, 50, 54, 58, 65, 66, 67, 72, 73, 76, 80, 83, 84, 86, 88, 89: AP/Wide World Photographs
Pages 15, 20, 36, 71: Courtesy Ellis Island Immigration Museum/NPS

Oral histories provided by Ellis Island Museum Oral History Project/National Park Service

A Creative Media Applications, Inc. Production

Project Coordinator: Matt Levine

Writers: Michael Burgan, Robin Doak, Matt Kachur, Joanne Mattern

Editors: Dorothy Anderson, Barbara Jean DiMauro, Kathleen White

Design and Production: Alan Barnett, Inc.

Associated Press Photo Researcher: Yvette Reyes

Ellis Island Librarian: Barry Moreno

Ellis Island Volunteer: David H. Cassells

Director, Ellis Island Museum Oral History Project: Paul E. Sigrist Jr.

Oral History Transcribers: Nancy Vega, John Murieillo, Ann Bunley, Elysa Matsew, Roger Herz

Oral History Typist: Andrew Frisch

American immigration
        p.   cm.
    Summary: An alphabetical reference work examining the background, statistics, reception, and current status of those groups who have immigrated to America throughout history.
    ISBN 0-7172-9283-5 (set : hardcover : alk. paper). — ISBN 0-7172-9284-3 (v. 1 : hardcover : alk. paper). — ISBN 0-7172-9285-1 (v. 2 : hardcover : alk. paper). — ISBN 0-7172-9286-X (v. 3 : hardcover : alk. paper)
    1. United States — Emigration and immigration — Juvenile literature — Encyclopedias. [1. United States — Emigration and immigration — Encyclopedias.] I. Grolier Educational Corporation.
    JV6450.A59   1999
    304.8'73 — dc21   99–18077
                                                                                CIP
                                                                                AC

Printed in the United States of America

Contents

PREFACE

Immigration has played an enormous role in the history of the United States. Numerous ethnic backgrounds have combined over the centuries of our country's existence, and in this modern time it is not unusual to find people who claim a variety of heritages yet still clearly think of themselves as American. Further, the contributions of other cultures to American society are countless. People in the United States are exposed every day to food, clothing, art, and language that have been strongly influenced by ideas from races and nations around the world.

In many ways the history of U.S. immigration tells the history of our country. This set explores U.S. immigration and tells the stories of those who have *emigrated,* or left their homelands, so they could *immigrate* to, or enter, the United States. All have come to America with one common goal: to better their lives in some manner in a new land.

The set has two introductory volumes—the first an overview of U.S. immigration, and the second a historical account of Ellis Island in New York, where millions of immigrants in the 19th and 20th centuries first set foot on American soil to be processed before they made their ways to their final destinations in this country. The volumes that follow are an encyclopedic reference on immigration topics and immigrant groups from A to Z. Entries about particular immigrant groups include locator maps. A dotted line on a map points to a specific country or continent from which an immigrant group has originated; a circle outlines a more general region from which an immigrant group has come. There are cross-references to related topics at the end of most entries in the box labeled *See also.* An icon of the Statue of Liberty appears with each *See also* box. Additionally, some main entry headings are followed only by cross-references to other entries (for example, ABOLITIONIST NEWSPAPERS— See LITERATURE, THE MEDIA, AND ETHNICITY). These cross-references direct readers to the entries containing the information they seek. (Cross-references are not used within the introductory volumes; the first two volumes have information that will naturally apply to all the entries in the A-to-Z volumes.) The set index, which is included at the back of each volume, also can help readers quickly find specific subjects within the set. A list of suggested further reading about immigration is provided as well for students to use for subsequent research.

To add to the richness of the subject matter, sidebars appear throughout the set, providing interesting facts and stories regarding immigrants and immigration. Transcripts of interviews from the Ellis Island Museum Oral History Project have also been included in the set. The interviews provide personal accounts of what it was like for those who chose to seek a new life in this country. The interviews are denoted by a ship icon to make them easy to locate. They were lightly edited for readability. Original language usage and spellings were retained in the numerous quotations cited throughout the set.

INTRODUCTION

About 50 years ago historian Oscar Handlin made a famous study of American immigrants called *The Uprooted* (1951). Handlin wrote, "Once I thought to write the history of immigrants in America. I discovered the immigrants *were* American history."

Immigrants are people who move. They leave their homelands, for a variety of reasons, and seek better lives in other countries. For more than 400 years millions of immigrants have reached the shores of America. Over the centuries many probably shared the feelings of William Bradford, one of the earliest of America's immigrants, when he and his fellow Pilgrims from the *Mayflower* landed in Massachusetts. Bradford wrote of their landing, "Being thus arrived in a good harbor and brought safe to land, they [the Pilgrims] fell upon their knees and blessed the God of heaven who had brought them over the vast and furious ocean...."

Bradford's Pilgrims and other immigrants from England came to America for religious and political freedom and economic opportunity. The first English immigrants were followed by about 400,000 more before the Revolutionary War (1775–1783). England's control of what became the United States led to an American culture that was largely Anglo, or English-influenced.

But long before the first English settlers came to the New World, ancestors of today's Native Americans had made the long trek from Asia to America. They had lived happily for thousands of years without knowing a thing about Europeans or their culture.

Contact with the Europeans resulted in the deaths of many Native Americans and destroyed their societies. Meanwhile, America became a meeting ground for different ethnic and racial groups from around the world.

Continuing through the 17th century, other Europeans joined the English settlers, although their numbers were much smaller. They also were looking for new freedom and better lives. Other early immigrants—black slaves from Africa—belonged to a different race than the white English majority. They had to confront *racism,* or the whites' belief that their race was superior to others. Carried over in chains on crowded ships, the Africans did not choose to become immigrants and were not likely to bless any god when they reached their new land.

The treatment of new arrivals by the dominant Anglo culture has often varied. When Americans needed cheap

This is a traditional painting of the landing of the Pilgrims at Plymouth Rock in 1620. More than three centuries later people are still "landing" in America.

labor and people to help settle the open lands of the West, they encouraged immigrants to come. Most Americans saw their country as a safe and welcoming place for people attacked for their political or religious beliefs at home. That feeling is illustrated in the poem engraved at the bottom of the Statue of Liberty. The work is called "The New Colossus," and its most famous line is: "'Give me your tired, your poor, / your huddled masses yearning to breathe free.'"

At the same time, members of the dominant American culture have often been suspicious and fearful of many immigrants. Perhaps the immigrants belonged to different religions, or were not Caucasians (whites), or simply seemed too "foreign" in their habits and beliefs. Prejudice and discrimination against immigrants have been constant themes in American history.

Because of that prejudice and discrimination, many immigrants have had a hard time adjusting to life in America. They want to become part of the dominant Anglo culture, or at least have a fair chance to make a good living and enjoy personal freedom. At the same time, they often want to keep their native languages and cultures. The struggle to belong has been even more difficult for nonwhite racial groups, because their physical differences— particularly their skin color—have stirred racism among many members of the white, Anglo culture. The challenge of becoming fully American while keeping ties to the homeland continues for today's immigrants, most of whom come from Latin America and Asia.

For many years Americans assumed their country was a "melting pot"— people from many different lands and ethnic and racial backgrounds easily blended or melted together to form a new ethnic group: the Americans. The national motto reflects that belief: *E pluribus unum,* Latin for "Out of many, one." Today, however, more people argue that Americans do and should keep their ties to their ethnic and racial heritages, while still sharing some common values, such as a belief in democracy and liberty.

The American people's attitudes toward immigration have changed constantly throughout the country's history. Despite many negative feelings toward immigrants at various times, immigrants have always found a way to fit into the country's culture. Individual immigrants and their children have become important inventors, politicians, business and labor leaders, and educators. Ethnic groups have added words to the English language; introduced music, dances, and festivals; and spiced up the American diet with foods that once seemed exotic, but now are common. People from many different, distant lands still help shape American culture, even as they struggle to adapt to the culture they find when they arrive.

Immigration was at the core of American history when Oscar Handlin wrote *The Uprooted*. Immigrants and what they bring to the United States are still at the center of the American experience today.

CHAPTER I
The First Arrivals

A Long Trek East

More than 30,000 years ago people from Asia headed eastward toward the edge of Siberia. At that time a land bridge connected Asia with Alaska, and tribes of early Asians walked across the bridge. The Asians—America's first immigrants—found a land where no humans lived. They came at the time of the last great ice age, when sheets of ice and snow up to 2 miles thick, called *glaciers,* covered most of Canada and parts of the United States.

The first settlers went south to avoid the ice. Over the centuries they moved back north as the ice melted. They probably lived in caves, although one historian says, "… it would be wrong to think of them as stereotypical 'cavemen,' with stooped shoulders, heavy brows, and dull, brutish features." The early peoples made clothes, tools, and weapons, and they had religious beliefs tied to the natural world. For food they hunted packs of wild animals— mastodons and other mammals that no longer exist. Eventually, the settlers and their descendants spread throughout North and South America.

From time to time the land bridge that linked Asia and America was covered by glaciers, cutting off the two continents. When the bridge appeared again, new waves of immigrants moved to the new lands. By about 3000 B.C. the land bridge disappeared for good. All the Asian settlers who crossed that bridge were the ancestors of the people we call Native Americans today. Although not technically immigrants— in their own minds or to some scholars—today's Native Americans have

their roots in other lands, just as the immigrants of more recent times do. For thousands of years the Native Americans had the continent of North America to themselves, and they maintained their religious bonds with the land, the plants, and the animals. When Europeans first came to North America, they brought different values; their cultures clashed with the beliefs of the Native Americans, leading to physical clashes as well.

Native-American singers and drummers of the Pueblo tribe celebrate in Santa Clara Pueblo, New Mexico, by making music the traditional way. The Pueblos have maintained their unique culture through the centuries.

New People from across the Ocean

The story of Christopher Columbus and his voyage to the New World is a familiar one. Columbus thought he had reached the East Indies by following a new route west from Europe. He called the native people he met "Indians." But almost 500 years before Columbus, another group of Europeans had reached North America and tried to settle there.

The Vikings, or Norsemen, had come from northern Europe and settled in Iceland and Greenland. From Greenland Leif Ericsson sailed toward North America and spotted a land he called Vinland. Later his brother Thorvald led an expedition to Vinland, which brought about the first meeting between Europeans and Native Americans. The encounter was not a peaceful one. The Vikings came upon a small group of natives and took all but one prisoner. That night the Native Americans attacked the strangers and killed Ericsson. Another group of Norsemen arrived later, but after more battles with the native people, the Europeans left for good.

The city of St Augustine, Florida, was founded in 1565 as a Spanish military outpost. Since then the city has endured siege, invasion, pirate raiding, fire, fever, and hurricane.

The story of Vinland was passed on orally by the Vikings until it was finally written down in the 14th and 15th centuries. In 1960 archaeologists found evidence that the Vikings had lived in what is now Newfoundland, Canada—the first known European settlement in North America. For many years some people claimed the Vikings had reached New England, but no proof has been found.

Although their presence did not affect the development of the United States, the Vikings were the first European immigrants to the New World. Their stormy relations with the Native Americans were an early indication of the future conflicts Europeans would have with the peoples they found in North America.

■ The Great Age of Explorers

Columbus and the other explorers of his era had not heard about the Viking discovery of Vinland. Europeans in the late 15th century did not know that the continents of North and South America lay more than 3,000 miles to the west, between Europe and Asia. That is why Columbus assumed he could sail west and reach China and the East Indies. His incomplete knowledge of geography—plus his courage to go where no other sailor of his time had gone before—changed world history. The discovery of two previously unknown continents led to a race to take the natural resources of those lands. In the process of seeking economic gain, the first European immigrants came to America.

When Columbus landed in what is now the Bahamas, he was working for Spain. Spain and Portugal were among the leading European powers of the day, and they competed to find trading opportunities in the lands beyond their continent. As the centuries passed, other countries—France, England, Holland, Russia, Sweden—joined the hunt for distant territories to control and tap for their natural wealth. The rulers of Europe sent explorers to the New

World to claim lands in their names. In some cases the royal governments formed special companies to start trading ventures. From the beginning North America attracted daring or desperate Europeans with the promise of economic success. Political and religious freedom later became other strong lures for immigrants.

The Spanish and the French in North America

The Spanish were the first to try to settle in North America. In 1521 the explorer Juan Ponce de Leon sailed with 200 men from Puerto Rico to the Gulf Coast of Florida. However, their expedition ended quickly when Native Americans drove them off. During the next 40 years the Spanish kept trying to colonize Florida, but each attempt failed. Finally, a frustrated King Philip II called an end to the efforts in 1561. The French then took the opportunity to send settlers to America.

In 1562 French Protestants called Huguenots first landed in Florida—their settlement ended up in what is now North Carolina. That settlement broke apart two years later, just before more Huguenot immigrants arrived in Florida. Not wanting to give up the territory to the French, the Spanish once again sent settlers to Florida. In 1565 fighting between the French and Spanish ended with a Spanish victory. The battles between the two European powers—as well as battles with local Native Americans—continued for many years. Eventually, the Spanish won control of the area.

The Spanish also turned their attention to the West. From their thriving colony in Mexico, Spanish settlers moved northward into what is now New Mexico. In 1598 they established the first European settlement in America west of the Mississippi River. In northern New Mexico the Spanish found Native Americans living in towns that featured huge homes made out of mud and straw, called *adobe*. The Spanish called those people Pueblo (Spanish for "town") Indians. As was the case in Florida, the Native Americans and the Spanish often battled before the Spanish took complete control.

The English Arrive

In the meantime the English showed their first interest in colonizing the Atlantic Coast of North America. In 1584 Sir Walter Raleigh led an expedition to Roanoke Island, off land he named Virginia. The next year settlers returned to Roanoke, but the colony—like the first Spanish and French colonies—did not last. More English settlers came to Roanoke, but the site was abandoned by 1591, with no trace of the missing settlers. During the short time of the Roanoke colony, Virginia

The road ahead leads in two different directions for a boy crossing a bridge in Taos, New Mexico. One path leads to life in the "white man's" culture; the other returns to the reservation. Today Native Americans are torn between the two cultures.

Dare was born. She was the first child of English parents born in America.

The Roanoke colony also led to the first English propaganda about the New World. One member of the first group wrote a book called *A Briefe and True Account of the New Found Land of Virginia* (1588). The book described the potential for settlement and trade in America, while largely ignoring the risks involved. For hundreds of years after, similar accounts would entice immigrants to leave Europe for America.

While the Roanoke settlement was trying to survive, the Spanish continued to move farther into the territory they claimed along the Atlantic Coast. (By that time the French had given up on Florida and shifted their attention to their lands in New France, or Canada.) The Spanish tried to convert the Native Americans to Christianity and had some success. However, their settlements generally did not extend north of St. Augustine—the first permanent settlement of European immigrants in America, established by the Spanish in 1565.

The English were still determined to have a presence in North America, and in 1606 two companies were formed to explore and settle the Atlantic Coast. The London Company focused on Virginia, while the Plymouth Company looked farther north, to New York and New England. In 1606 the London Company sent out three ships that would finally establish a permanent English colony in America.

The Native Americans of Florida

By some estimates, about 2.5 million people lived in what are now the United States and Canada when Columbus reached the New World. Two decades later, when Juan Ponce de Leon tried to settle in Florida, he encountered the Calusa—natives of the region. Based on the Gulf Coast, the Calusa influence spread across Florida to the Atlantic Ocean. They constructed canals to travel through the swampy interior lands and made artificial islands out of seashells, then built their towns on them.

The Spanish guaranteed themselves a hostile greeting from the Calusa when they began raiding the shore and taking the Native Americans as slaves. When the Spanish tried to start a colony, the Calusa attacked. For decades afterward, the Spanish and the Calusa battled each other. Eventually, the Spanish left the Calusa alone, and in the 17th century the Native Americans established friendlier ties with the Spanish based in Cuba. Foreign diseases, however, killed many of the Calusa, just as European illnesses sparked deadly epidemics among other Native-American nations.

CHAPTER 2
Jamestown and Beyond

The First Colony

On May 24, 1607, English settlers from the London Company founded Jamestown in Virginia. Despite struggling through its early years, the town eventually became the first permanent English settlement in North America. The colonists, led by John Smith, faced disease and starvation during their first few months in Virginia. Like all the original European immigrants, their lives depended largely on what they brought with them or could make in America. In the first year, however, that was usually not enough to survive. Luckily for the English in Jamestown, a local Native-American tribe, the Powhatan, brought corn and bread. Later, according to Smith, "With fish, oysters, bread and deer they kindly traded with me and my men." (The Native Americans of New England were just as generous, helping the Pilgrims survive their first winter in Plymouth.)

Despite the food from the Powhatan, half of the Jamestown settlers died by September. Most of the survivors were too sick to work. To add to the settlers' problems, relations with the Native Americans soon turned sour. During the first few decades after the English arrived, they often clashed with the Powhatan, then had periods of uneasy peace. As more settlers came, the Native Americans feared—correctly—that they would lose their lands. Generally, the English felt themselves superior to the "savage" Native Americans and did not hesitate to take those lands.

Thanks to their superior weapons, the diseases they carried, and the constant stream of new arrivals, the English were able to dominate the Native Americans, either killing them or forcing them to move westward. After the English established colonies along the East Coast, new immigrants from Europe had to adapt to the English way of life. Even people who did accept that culture often had problems adapting to life in America.

Slaves and Indentured Servants

The English were not the only ethnic group to reach Jamestown. In his account of life in Virginia, John Smith noted that Poles and Dutchmen (the English term for Germans) had come with them, hired to make soap, glass, and other essentials of life. Immigrants were also recorded from other lands, such as a few "Switzers," from Switzerland, and one "Martin the Armenian," who came around 1619.

That same year the racial mix of Jamestown changed when a Dutch

To guard themselves against raids from hostile forces, the first settlers at Jamestown in 1607 built three-cornered forts. Within the forts were small, thatched houses which were protected by guns at the three bulwarks.

trading ship arrived with 20 Africans. In the 16th century the Spanish and Portuguese had begun buying African slaves and bringing them to work in their new colonies. The other European nations soon followed that practice. The Jamestown Africans, however, were most likely indentured servants, not slaves.

Not Slaves, but Not Free

To the people who owned their contracts, *indentured servants* (immigrants who agreed to work for a period of time, usually between four and seven years, in return for passage to America) were valuable assets. "Our principle wealth," wrote one Virginia plantation owner, "consisteth in servants." The servants were often convicts; one historian says many were "raked from the gutter." Most were men who came without their families. White and black servants worked side by side, clearing fields and planting tobacco. Sometimes they were forced to wear metal collars around their necks, and if they refused to obey their masters, they were whipped.

Given the harsh life, it is not surprising that many servants ran away. Masters placed ads in local newspapers seeking such runaways. One master composed his ad in rhyme:

Last Wednesday noon, at break of day,

From Philadelphia ran away

An Irishman named John McKeoghn,

To fraud and imposition prone;

About five feet, five inches high,

Can curse and swear as well as lie...."

For Africans indentured servitude quickly gave way to slavery. By the 1650s an estimated 70 percent of the blacks in Virginia were slaves. Racist attitudes among the English made it easy for them to enslave blacks. For whites indentured servitude lasted through the 18th century.

Indentured servants signed contracts to work for their masters for a set number of years—usually from four to seven. Their contracts could be sold from one master to another, so the servants were treated as property, as slaves were. But after finishing their terms of service, the indentured servants were free—most slaves remained in

slavery their whole lives. Both whites and blacks arrived in America as indentured servants. In the 17th century about 75 percent of the immigrants came as indentured servants. Over time most of the blacks who came to Virginia and the other English colonies nearby were slaves. By 1750 about 250,000 Africans and their descendants were living in America; most were slaves.

■ Settlement to the North

The Virginia colony had been started primarily as a business venture. The English who arrived in Massachusetts in 1620, the Pilgrims, also wanted to go into business—by setting up a trading post. But their religious beliefs were what had led them out of England, first to Holland and then to America. Not all the people who arrived on the *Mayflower* were Separatists, as the religious Pilgrims called themselves. (The Separatists had separated from the major English religion of the time, the Anglican Church.) However, the Separatist philosophy came to dominate the Plymouth Plantation, the original settlement of the Pilgrims.

About a decade later English settlers called Puritans also landed in Massachusetts. Their name came from their desire to purify the Anglican Church without separating from it. They shared some goals with the Pilgrims: ending most church rituals and any beliefs that were not based on the Bible; setting up individual churches, or congregations, that ran their own affairs; and living simple, moral lives as members of God's "chosen people." The Puritans believed they could be good Christians and successful business owners in America. As their leader,

John Winthrop, put it, they would be "a city on a hill" that served as a model for the world to follow.

For both the Puritans and the Pilgrims, establishing social order and a government was important, and both drew upon English political ideas and their own religious beliefs to create democratic self-rule—democratic for the members of their faith, at least. People who did not accept Puritan or Separatist ideas were not allowed to vote on local affairs.

The strict religious nature of the Massachusetts colonies—and the ones that sprang from them in Connecticut—was not appealing to most immigrants. One historian says, "The New England people, almost to a man, were English and Puritan." Into the early 19th century the region did not attract as many non-English immigrants as the other colonies did. New England also did not rely on slaves or indentured servants the way Virginia and the other southern colonies did. Southern farmers grew their crops— mostly rice and tobacco (and later cotton)—on large farms that required many workers. The New England farms were smaller, and more of the economy was based on the making and trading of goods. By 1700 New England had perhaps only 1,000 Africans, and most were indentured servants.

◼ Other Faiths in the Colonies

Puritans and Pilgrims dominated in New England, while Virginia settlers were mostly members of the Anglican Church, which was also a Protestant faith. The early Protestant groups were followed to America by people of other faiths. The Protestants did not accept the practices and beliefs of the other religions or the people who lived by them. In many cases old tensions that had developed in England came with the settlers to America.

Roman Catholics

During the 16th century in England, Roman Catholics and Protestants had fought each other, and the Protestants had won. By the 17th century the Catholics were a minority in England and were often treated harshly by the Protestants.

George Calvert, Lord Baltimore, was a Catholic noble. When he tried to gain lands in Virginia in the early 1630s, he received a hostile reception because of his religion. Calvert then asked King Charles I for his own colony where he could grow tobacco. Calvert soon died, so his sons Cecilius and Leonard received lands granted by the king, just north of Virginia. The Calverts set up a colony there in 1634 and called it

Above is a copy of an oil painting depicting the Pilgrims' first Thanksgiving in Plymouth.

Maryland. George Calvert had wanted his land to be a safe place for Catholics, and it was. But the Calverts also welcomed Protestants, and in 1649 Maryland passed a law officially accepting Christians of all faiths. (Rhode Island, under the Protestant rebel Roger Williams, had an even more tolerant position, accepting Jews as well.)

Racial Slaughter in New England

Land and independence were at the heart of one of the bloodiest North American struggles between Europeans and Native Americans. King Philip's War lasted for more than a year, and when it was over the English had guaranteed their dominance over the Native Americans of New England.

King Philip was the English name for Metacom, the leader of the Pokanoket tribe. In 1662 the leaders of Plymouth forced Metacom to sign a treaty saying the English had to give their approval before the Pokanoket sold any land. Over the years the English took even more control over the Pokanoket and neighboring tribes. In July 1675 a frustrated Metacom led an attack on New England towns in Rhode Island and Massachusetts. Fighting between Native Americans and the English broke out elsewhere in New England as well.

"The bullets seemed to fly like hail," one survivor wrote, as the natives burned houses, killed hundreds, and took prisoners. In all, twelve towns were destroyed. The English fought back with their own rampages and assaults. Thousands died in the fighting. The war ended when Metacom was captured and beheaded in August 1676. His head was kept on public display in Plymouth for 25 years—a grisly reminder that the Native Americans were defeated and were now inferior people in their own land.

Maryland's acceptance of Protestants eventually led to the end of Catholicism as the colony's dominant religion. After squabbles within the Catholic community and between Catholics and Protestants, the English government took control, and in 1692 it made the Anglican Church the official church of the colony. For the most part few Catholics, either from England or other countries, came to the English colonies after that point until the early 19th century.

Early Protestants in Pennsylvania

Another religious minority in England was the Quakers. Formally called the Religious Society of Friends, the Quakers got their nickname because some early members trembled as they prayed, moved by their deep faith. They shared some beliefs with the Puritans, but they also had some unique ideas of their own. The Quakers were strongly opposed to violence and refused to fight under any circumstances. In their religious services the members of the congregation sat silently until someone felt an urge to speak. The Puritans and Anglicans disliked the Quakers, and in the American colonies such Protestants refused to let the Quakers worship as they wanted.

William Penn, a wealthy Quaker, wanted to start an American colony where Quakers would have religious freedom. In 1681 he received territory from King Charles II as payment for a debt the crown owed his family. Penn's colony was named Pennsylvania, and it welcomed people of all faiths. The Quakers also had friendly relations with the Native Americans in the colony and opposed slavery. Penn's most important policy, at least relating to immigration, was recruiting Germans to help settle his new land.

Some groups of German Protestants did not belong to the official churches of their homelands and faced discrimination as a result. The promise of religious freedom lured those people to Pennsylvania. They were joined by German-speaking Swiss and some Dutch. In 1683 the first group of Germans arrived in the colony, and they soon started their own community: Germantown. By the early 1700s

Germans were streaming into Pennsylvania.

The Germans joined a small number of other non-English-speaking settlers, mostly Swedes and Finns. Those Scandinavians were already in Pennsylvania before Penn took control. They had come to the colony of New Sweden—which was located in present-day Delaware—during the mid-17th century. Another major immigrant group entering Pennsylvania was the Scotch-Irish. Those Protestants had moved from Scotland to Ireland in the 16th and 17th centuries. Many then moved on to America in the 18th century. The Scotch-Irish settled mostly in Pennsylvania, Virginia, and the Carolinas. One immigrant wrote to his family in Dublin that Pennsylvania was "...the best country for working folk and tradesmen of any in the world."

◼ Other Europeans in America

In addition to the English—and later the Germans and Scotch-Irish—other groups of Europeans made their marks on America during the days of colonization.

The French

During the 17th century France was England's major rival in North America. But where the English tended to form permanent colonies that attracted many settlers, the French presence in what is now the United States was not as great. After abandoning their settlement in Florida in 1580, the French focused their colonial efforts in Canada. When they did journey into America, they usually came down from the north, along the Great Lakes or into the Mississippi Valley. Their major city in

America was New Orleans, which was not founded until 1701. Before then the French lived mostly in small settlements set up for fur trapping and trading.

One particular group of French immigrants did come in large numbers to North America, but they settled in English territory. The Huguenots were French Protestants who held religious beliefs similar to the Puritans'. In 1685 King Louis XIV of France repealed a law that gave the Huguenots religious freedom in France, which was mostly Catholic. Up to 15,000 Huguenots eventually came to America; most settled in the New York area and South Carolina. The Huguenots were mostly well educated and had useful business skills. They quickly adapted to the English culture in America.

Dutch, Swedes, and Finns

The Netherlands, a small country in northern Europe, was a major commercial power in the 17th century. The people from that land, the Dutch, first explored North America in 1609.

Labor Day is not a day of rest for everybody, as these three Amish farmers bring in a load of harvested corn from their Bird In Hand, Pennsylvania, farm.

That year Henry Hudson—an English captain working for the Netherlands—explored the river in New York that now bears his name. Within 15 years the Dutch had their first permanent colony, which they called New Netherland. By 1630 the colony's largest trading post, New Amsterdam, had about 300 citizens. However, the colony did not remain under Dutch control for long. In 1664 the English took it over, renaming the territory New York. The city of New Amsterdam became New York City.

Another northern European nation wanted a colony in North America in the 17th century. In March 1638 a group of Swedes, along with some Finns, landed at what is now Wilmington, Delaware, and established the colony of New Sweden. The colony never numbered more than 500 people, and by 1655 it was struggling to survive. That year the Dutch took over New Sweden, making it part of New Netherland. Some of the descendants of the original Swedish and Finnish immigrants ended up in Pennsylvania.

Today the states of Pennsylvania, New York, New Jersey, Delaware, and Maryland are called the Middle Atlantic states. In the 17th century that region had the greatest ethnic diversity in America, and that trend continued during the 18th century. But even as settlers from many lands filled those colonies, one country was in control: England. After the French and Indian War with France (1756–1763) England owned land from Canada to Florida. Thirteen colonies were in place, and English culture and language dominated America.

CHAPTER 3
The New Nation and Immigrants

■ Revolution!

When the Revolutionary War (1775–1783) broke out, about 2.5 million people lived in the 13 colonies (not counting Native Americans). About one-fifth were Africans and their descendants. Of the white Americans, most were English. Many immigrants from other countries were also British subjects, since they had been *naturalized* (given citizenship rights) either in England or in the colonies. Other immigrants, such as the Scots and the Irish, were already British subjects. Members of all the different ethnic groups shared a sense of outrage when the British attempted to increase control over their lives in America.

But even among the English Americans, not everyone supported the war for independence. John Adams, one of the revolution's leaders, suggested that the colonies were roughly split into thirds: one-third for the war, one-third against, and one-third neutral. The division arose among ethnic groups as well. The largest non-English ethnic groups were the Scotch-Irish and the Germans, and members of both groups either opposed independence or actively aided the British. The Scotch-Irish, one historian suggests, did not want to risk losing newly acquired lands by opposing the English crown. While German immigrant soldiers comprised a large part of General George Washington's private guard, other Germans around Philadelphia sold food to the British. Some Germans avoided taking sides because they opposed the war on religious grounds.

Still, immigrants with roots in various countries did make crucial contributions to the war for independence. Paul Revere was the descendant of a French Huguenot named Apollon Rivoir. One-fifth of the members of the Continental Congress, the body that signed the Declaration of Independence, came from Scotland. Charles Carroll, an Irish Catholic, also signed that historic document. Another Irish immigrant, Captain John Barry, captured a number of British ships during naval battles and was later called the father of the American Navy. Both

Mexico's California

During the years that England gained control of the eastern part of America—and then lost it to the new United States—Spain continued to settle the Southwest. In 1769 two expeditions left Mexico to start religious missions in what is now California. The Spanish feared that the British and Russians would claim that land first. (Russians eventually did build a fort and small community near San Francisco, bringing Russian immigrants to the region.)

By that time Spaniards had been living in Mexico for almost 250 years. The upper classes mostly had Spanish roots, but many Mexicans had Native-American ancestry as well. Many of the poorer Mexicans were the first settlers in California. Few people wanted to come north to that new land. The governor tried to entice immigrants with the following report: "This is a great country, the most peaceful and quiet in the world … [with] good bread, excellent meat, and tolerable fish."

When Mexico declared its independence from Spain in 1821, only about 3,000 Mexicans lived in California. Most were the descendants of the original settlers, and they supported the new Mexican government. They also welcomed Americans into their lands as immigrants, although after 1841 the Mexicans thought the Americans who came were too greedy. In 1846 the United States and Mexico began the Mexican-American War (1846–1848) over U.S. control of Texas and American interest in other Mexican territory. The next year in the midst of the war, the U.S. government took control of California and other southwestern lands where Mexicans lived.

free blacks and slaves fought for the Patriots; some slaves were given their freedom in return for their service. Among the Native Americans, most supported the English or remained neutral, but Oneida natives extended important aid. During the harsh winter of 1777–1778 at Valley Forge, Pennsylvania, they donated blankets and corn to Washington's troops.

The First Census

The Constitution requires the government to conduct a census, or a count, of the population every ten years. But the U.S. Census Bureau does more than count bodies; it also asks questions about the social and economic conditions of Americans.

The first census, in 1790, reported 3,929,214 Americans. About one-fifth of those people (approximately 750,000) were Africans and their descendants. (Native Americans were not counted at that time.) Using census information, historians have made an estimate of the ethnic or language backgrounds for white Americans in 1790.

National Origin	Percent of White Population
English	60.9
Scottish	8.3
Irish/Scotch-Irish	9.7
German	8.7
Dutch	3.4
French	1.7
Swedish (includes Finns)	0.7
Other/Unknown	6.6

SOURCE: *Coming to America* (1990)

◼ Building a Nation

After its victory over the British in 1783, the new United States of America had to grapple with creating an effective government. The first governing system tried by the United States used the Articles of Confederation, and under those articles each state was considered independent but united with the others in a "firm league of friendship." But the national government was too weak to be effective under that system. The new

government developed in 1787 addressed that problem. Meeting in Philadelphia, 55 of the young nation's top political leaders created the Constitution, spelling out the workings of the U.S. government.

The Constitution

Immigration is not specifically addressed in the Constitution, although the delegates at the convention did consider it. Some, like George Mason, were for "opening a wide door for emigrants." Others, however, feared immigrants would bring political ideas from their homelands that were not compatible with democracy. In the end the Constitution allowed any foreign-born citizen to hold any political office except the presidency and vice presidency. The document also gave Congress the authority to draft laws concerning naturalization, so foreigners could become citizens. Congress passed its first law of that kind in 1790, making naturalization relatively easy for immigrants as long as they were white; racial restrictions on naturalization lasted into the 1950s. Any white person born in America was automatically a citizen—but Native Americans and slaves were not recognized as citizens. The citizenship status of free blacks was not specified, but they were often denied the right to vote and faced other discriminatory laws.

Fear of the French

After the beginning of the French Revolution (1789–1799) political conditions in Europe were unsettled. American opinion was divided regarding whether or not to support the new French government. Some Americans called for stricter naturalization laws to prevent immigrants—especially the French and Irish—from becoming involved in American politics. One journalist expressed the fears of the anti-immigrant forces; he wrote that unless the country restricted the participation of undesirable newcomers, "… the peace and the liberties of this country must fall a sacrifice to the passions and the politics of foreigners."

Congress responded to the concern with a series of laws aimed at restricting the rights of *aliens*—citizens of other countries living in America—and made it harder for them to become naturalized Americans. The debate over the laws was heated and even turned violent. A cartoon from 1798 shows two congressmen, one for the laws and one against, battling each other in the House of Representatives. The laws, called the Alien and Sedition Acts, marked the first effort by the government to limit the rights of immigrants.

■ Into the 19th Century

The turmoil in Europe led to war, caused by the rise of France's Napoléon Bonaparte and his desire to take over neighboring lands. The wars slowed immigration to America. During that period in 1803 the United States bought the Louisiana Territory from Napoléon—now French immigrants who had settled in the territory were under American rule. (A similar situation occurred again in 1819, when the government acquired Florida from Spain.)

In 1808 the importing of slaves was outlawed in America; slave owners had to rely on the children of existing American slaves to increase their holdings. Some slave traders, however, managed to smuggle slaves into the country.

Without the arrival of new immigrants from Europe, the existing immigrants were slowly cut off from their old cultures. They assimilated by adopting the language and habits of Anglo Americans. That process was also sometimes called "Americanization," a term first used in the middle of the 19th century. Generally, when the number of foreign arrivals was higher, the members of different ethnic groups had more chances to speak their native languages, keep old traditions alive, and build immigrant communities that were largely separate from the dominant American culture.

Below is an etching of immigrants aboard a ship in 1850.

The Push and Pull of Immigration

After 1815, when peace came to Europe and the United States ended another war with Britain—the War of 1812 (1812–1815)—the pace of immigration slowly began to rise. Immigration was largely the result of two forces. Factors in Europe "pushed" people to seek a better life elsewhere. The push could be related to politics or religion, but usually it sprang from economics. On the other side of the Atlantic Ocean the potential for economic success in America "pulled" the immigrants as well. Such push and pull factors varied over time and were not always equal, but some combination of them brought most immigrants to America.

In Europe part of the push was a population boom and the resulting shortage of food. Europe's population doubled between 1750 and 1850, and many people had a difficult time finding good farmland or jobs that paid well.

America's primary pull was its abundance of cheap land. Immigrants could move west and clear their own plots to farm. The life on the frontier was difficult, but the rewards were great for successful farmers. For skilled workers another pull was jobs that offered higher wages than those in Europe. Once some members of an ethnic group settled in the United States, they usually wrote back to their friends and family about the opportunities they found. The so-called America letters increased the pull on Europeans to come to America.

In 1816 a Welsh farmer living in New York wrote about what he had found in America. He talked of the high wages at a shipyard in Albany and the lack of poverty in the region: "We have not seen one poor person begging since we have been here and that is 13 years." He told his relatives to come to America: "I would be glad to see thousands of you and still be able to say that there is room."

The Government and the Immigrants

For the most part the U.S. government took a "hands-off" approach toward immigration during much of the 19th century. Individual states handled the arrival of immigrants, collecting taxes to help pay for their medical inspections and to aid the poor. But in 1819 Congress passed the Passenger Act to try to regulate the conditions immigrants endured on their voyages to the United States.

Most immigrants were poor and they arrived on ships packed with hundreds of passengers. Traveling by sail, the trip could take up to two months—even much longer if weather was very bad—and rough seas often rocked the wooden vessels. Below decks people sometimes slept two to a bunk, and they faced deadly diseases and bad food—when they received enough to eat at all. The Passenger Act limited the number of passengers on board ships arriving in America and spelled out how much food and water the ships had to carry. The law did not completely end the suffering during the Atlantic crossing, but it eased the trip somewhat.

The 1819 law was also important for helping officials keep track of who was coming to America. For the first time the U.S. government required every ship's captain to submit a list of all passengers, giving their name, sex, occupation, age, and the country they came from. In the decade from 1821 to 1830 almost 99,000 Europeans immigrated to America. Another 44,000 came from other parts of the world, or their countries of origin were not listed. The largest ethnic group was the Irish, with more than 50,000 immigrants. In the years to follow the Irish and the Germans were the largest ethnic groups to come to America.

CHAPTER 4
The First Immigration "Explosion"

America Calls

The United States entered the 1840s as a growing economic power. The country was beginning to *industrialize,* or build large factories and mills to produce goods. The industrialization was most obvious in the Northeast. At the same time, settlers were pushing farther west, opening up new farmlands. Some politicians talked of the country's "manifest destiny," its God-given right to control all the territory it could. For the most part Americans welcomed the immigrants who came to the United States at the time, since their labor would help the nation grow.

In Europe the introduction of railroads made it easier for potential immigrants to reach ports and sail for America. Still, typical immigrants needed good reasons to leave their homes and make the difficult trip across the Atlantic Ocean.

For many Irish the reason was crop failure and famine. When agricultural disaster struck, hundreds of thousands of Irish joined their countrymen who had already gone to America. Many Germans also faced famine, while some left their homelands for political and religious reasons, or had skills that were in demand in the United States. Poor, rural workers in other countries left farms for jobs in growing European cities. The number of jobs, however, was often smaller than the number of job seekers, and the disappointed people then sailed for America. All such newcomers formed part of the first great wave of immigration, which lasted until the outbreak of the Civil War (1861–1865).

The Irish

The Irish came to America almost as soon as the English established colonies there. The early Irish immigrants included poor indentured servants (immigrants who agreed to work for a period of time, usually between four and seven years, in return for passage to the United States), free men, and even some wealthy leaders, such as Sir Thomas Dongan. In 1682 Dongan was named governor of New York. But Irish immigration exploded in the 19th century. Even before the peak years of the 1840s and 1850s, young Irish men went to the United States to work, taking such jobs as digging New York's Erie Canal. The Irish provided much of the back-breaking labor used to build roads and railways as well.

Although the Irish came from a rural country where most people worked on farms, in the United States they usually lived in cities where housing was cheap and jobs were plentiful. Boston and New York had large Irish populations, and the immigrants tended to live together in Irish neighborhoods. They developed a reputation for being *clannish,* or living and associating mostly with other Irish.

In 1835 one observer noted that Irish Americans often voted for other Irish immigrants or their descendants. "There is no election in any of the large cities without some previous calls upon the 'true-born sons of Ireland' to vote so or so." The Irish were not the only group to vote along ethnic lines, but they became the symbol of urban "machine" politics, where voters showed great loyalty to leaders from their own ethnic groups. In return the leaders found the voters jobs or helped them when family members became sick or died.

Battle over the Bible

In 1844 Protestants and Catholics—mostly Irish immigrants—battled in the streets of Philadelphia. The immediate cause was the use of the Catholic Bible in the public schools, but anti-Catholicism had been building in the city for years. On May 7 a Protestant mob entered an Irish neighborhood, crying, "Kill them, kill them!" During the riot that followed two Catholic churches were destroyed and 14 people were killed or wounded. Another riot two months later left another 13 people dead. Native-born Americans, however, were not totally to blame for the riots, as the Irish immigrants' hatred for the English and their American descendants added to the violence.

Through the 1850s violence continued against Catholics and their churches. At least a dozen churches were burned and many others were vandalized. In 1854 a priest in Portland, Maine, wrote, "Twice within the past month I have been stoned by young men…. I am hissed and insulted with vile language…." He noted that when the neighborhood children insulted him, the adults nearby smiled with approval.

Anti-Irish Sentiments

Many native-born Americans disliked the Irish clannishness. Americans with English roots were prejudiced against the Irish; they tended to share the English attitude that most Irish were lazy, dirty, and stupid. The Irish also had a longstanding hatred of the English. England had ruled Ireland for hundreds of years and the English often had treated the Irish brutally. The hatred between the Irish and the English carried over to America.

Adding to the tension were religious differences: most Anglo-Americans were Protestant, and most Irish immigrants of the 19th century were Roman Catholic. To the dominant Protestants, Catholics could not be trusted because they owed their loyalty to the leader of their church—the pope—in Rome. Some American Protestants feared Irish

Catholics would try to ruin the country's democratic values and push for laws that supported Catholic views. Other Catholic immigrants faced similar suspicions, but the Irish were the main targets during the middle of the 19th century since they were arriving in such large numbers. The native-born Americans who opposed Irish immigration, or immigration in general, were called *nativists*.

The large-scale Irish immigration led nativists to take action. In the 1830s some Americans began calling for more restrictions on immigration, or for extending the waiting period before immigrants could become *naturalized* (become citizens). At the time the waiting period was five years; the nativists wanted to make it 21 years. Political parties formed to try to make such ideas the law of the land. The prejudice against the Irish, and Catholics in general, sometimes led to violence. In 1834 a mob in Charlestown, Massachusetts, burned a convent. A decade later riots broke out in Philadelphia between Irish Catholics and American Protestants. (See "Battle over the Bible" sidebar.) The anti-Irish feelings grew alongside Irish immigration.

The "Great Hunger"

After 1845 one event in Ireland led to mass emigration. The so-called "great hunger" was caused by a disease that virtually wiped out Ireland's potato crop. The poor of Ireland relied on the potato as their main food; without it, thousands starved. Those who could leave Ireland did, and from 1845 to 1860 about 1.5 million Irish headed to America.

Like many of the Irish immigrants before them, the people fleeing the potato famine were mostly uneducated and poor. Once in the United States, they lacked money to move farther west, as many Germans and Scandinavians did, and so remained in the cities of the Northeast. Boston became a major Irish city; in 1850 people born in Ireland made up slightly more than 25 percent of the city's population of almost 137,000. Irish men continued to take jobs digging ditches and working in construction while the women took jobs as servants—when they could. *No Irish need apply* was a common phrase on help-wanted ads of the day.

The new Irish arrivals came from a land of death and poverty, due to the famine. In the United States they still faced poverty—and prejudice as well—but they had opportunities to advance, and many took advantage of those chances. Their large numbers in cities such as Boston and New York led to political power and city jobs—for example, working for the fire and police departments. And not all Americans looked down on the Irish. In the middle of the nativist feelings of the 1850s, Orestes Brownson defended them. A wealthy Bostonian, Brownson was a Protestant who became a Catholic and criticized the Americans who opposed his new religion. He also pointed out the virtues of the Irish. "Visit their families," Brownson wrote, "and you feel that you are in a pure and healthy atmosphere, and your hearts are melted by a love of parents to children, of children to parents, of brothers and sisters for each other, that you have never found in the families of Puritan origin."

Irish immigration to America peaked in the 1850s, when more than 900,000 arrived. Still, the end of the famine did not end Irish immigration; hundreds of thousands came every decade until the 1930s. New arrivals had family members in the United States, and the country continued to offer better job opportunities than Ireland did. In the 1990s about 40 million Americans claimed some Irish ancestry—second only to those who claimed some German ancestry. However, Irish Americans have kept a stronger sense of their ethnic identity than most Germans have. Ireland's past troubles—the famine and the country's difficult relations with England—have given many Irish Americans a deep pride in their ability to overcome hardship.

■ The Germans

Like the Irish, the Germans began coming to America in large numbers during the 1840s and 1850s. At the time Germany was not a united nation; there were a number of European countries with German-speaking populations. In 1848, after failed revolutions in some of those states, many Germans left their homelands to find greater freedom in the United States. Such Germans were sometimes referred to as "Forty-Eighters." Some left to escape a potato famine, although the famine was not as terrible as the one in Ireland. But on the whole most Germans came looking for better jobs or farmlands, and for the rest of the 19th century they were the largest immigrant group to come to America.

Unlike the Irish, who usually stayed in the cities of the Northeast, the Germans spread out in a wide geographic area. Many went to Pennsylvania, as the first German immigrants had. Others moved farther out west to the cities of St. Louis,

Chicago, and Cincinnati, or to the open spaces of the Midwest, where they could farm as they had in Europe.

As immigrants traveled west, they often rode in groups of covered wagons, as shown in the above print.

Germans belonged to all three major European religions of the day: Protestant, Catholic, and Jewish. Members of some smaller Protestant churches came to America so they could have freedom to worship as they pleased. The German Catholics were often the victims of the same anti-Catholic feelings the Irish faced. German Jews, who came in large numbers after 1848, were usually well educated and belonged to the middle class; they blended in with other successful Germans. Although Jews in America always experienced some anti-Semitism—prejudice because they were Jewish—the German Jews did not face the extreme anti-Semitic hatred that arose later in the 19th century. A newspaper editorial in 1854 praised the German Jews: "They are among the best, most orderly, well-disposed of our citizens."

In general, most native-born Americans respected Germans of every religion for their beliefs in hard work and dedication to their families. They were, however, sometimes criticized for remaining apart from Anglo-Americans and not learning English. Still, when midwestern states such as Wisconsin and Iowa were looking for new settlers, they actively recruited Germans to come to their lands.

■ Other Immigrants of the Era

Throughout the mid-19th century many immigrants continued to arrive from England, Scotland, and Wales, although not in the same huge numbers as the Irish and Germans. The British immigrants had an easy time *assimilating* (adopting) the Anglo-American culture. They did not stand out like the Irish, who practiced an unpopular religion, or the Germans, who spoke a foreign language. Since Great Britain had begun to create industries earlier than the United States had, it had many experienced factory workers. The mostly English and Scottish workers often found they could get higher wages in the new mills of America. Smaller numbers of English immigrants turned to farming, while more worked in skilled "white-collar" professions, such as medicine and law.

In 1851 an English immigrant who had been in America for four years wrote home to an English newspaper. He praised the life he found and noted that "there is less cause of complaint made against the English for misconduct or unruliness than against any other class of emigrants."

The Scandinavians

From the founding of the United States until the 1840s, few immigrants arrived from Scandinavia—Norway, Sweden, and Denmark. Although their numbers increased during the 1840s, they were only a small part of the European movement to America. Still, the Scandinavians played important roles in the areas where they settled; they opened large sections of forested land to farming.

More so than most other immigrant groups, the Scandinavians usually chose one occupation—farming—and settled almost exclusively in one area: the Midwest (particularly Minnesota, Wisconsin, Iowa, and Illinois). Yet some Scandinavians did live in cities. By 1900 Chicago had the second-largest Swedish population of any city in the world.

The greatest numbers of Swedish, Norwegian, and Danish immigrants came after the Civil War (the Danes were always the smallest group of the three), but even before the war they were helping to settle the Midwest. Like the Germans, they were sometimes recruited by state governments and railroad companies.

According to a study by a Danish scholar, the Scandinavian immigrants were often better educated than the people who stayed behind. Many of the literate newcomers sent letters back to their homelands, praising the life they found in America. In 1858 a Swedish minister wrote home telling people to come to Minnesota. He said he lived in a "flourishing town," and "even the poorest man is welcome; within a short time even his prospects may become bright if he is industrious."

The Chinese

While most of the immigration between 1840 and the Civil War came from Europe, one Asian ethnic group began to enter the United States in significant numbers. After the discovery of gold in California in 1848, the Chinese came to mine gold. Just 35 Chinese arrived in the 1840s, but from 1851 to 1860 the number of Chinese immigrants grew to more than 41,000. Most were single men, and they usually had to borrow money to come, taking part in a system similar to indentured servitude (a system where an immigrant agreed to work for a period of time, usually between four and seven years, in return for passage to the United States).

Most Chinese arrived in San Francisco and stayed in and around that city. The first Chinatown, or mostly Chinese community, was founded there. Although lured by the temptation of finding gold, few of the immigrants struck it rich. Mining of various minerals, however, remained a major occupation. Later the Chinese played a large part in building the railroads of the West. Often the Chinese—like other immigrants—took whatever jobs they could find at any wages. Many of them started laundries since few women came west for the gold rush, and American men were reluctant to do what was considered "women's work." The Chinese saw the laundries and other service jobs as a chance to make a good living in the United States.

When only a few Chinese were in America, most native-born citizens did not see them as any kind of threat. In 1850 one observer called them dignified and said, "They seem never to intervene or meddle in the affairs of others." But as their numbers grew, the Chinese faced some of the worst prejudice and discrimination directed against immigrants during the 19th century. (See Chapter 6.)

▪ Common Experiences

Wherever they came from, most of the immigrants of the first major wave shared some common experiences. Their trips across the ocean were usually in steerage, on the lowest decks of a ship. European immigrants usually arrived at one of five ports. (See "Where Immigrants Arrived" sidebar.) Some Irish landed first in Canada, then made their way south to the United States—often on foot.

Fighting "American Fever"

As early as the 1830s Norwegians seemed gripped by "American fever"—the desire to immigrate to the United States. Government officials and other leaders feared the drain of able-bodied citizens to America. One minister wrote a long letter to his congregation in 1837, warning of the "phantom of happiness in the American forests."

The voyage to America, he wrote, could be deadly. "Still another ship has sunk" with 200 dead, he reported, quoting a newspaper. Another ship carrying 180 immigrants arrived in New York with 30 people dead from starvation. "The passengers who still were alive when the ship arrived," he continued, "were in a most wretched plight." If the immigrants did arrive safely, they had to "work unceasingly, with the greatest exertion, and with almost no prospects of getting homes of their own or of acquiring fixed property."

At the time the "American fever" must have looked worse than it really was. In the 1840s only about 14,000 people came to the United States from Norway and Sweden combined. But in the decades to follow, more Norwegians did ignore the warnings and come to America—more than half a million arrived between 1861 and 1910.

At the port, the immigrants' first view of their new home revealed bustling docks. For most newcomers the air was filled with a foreign language. The immigrants arrived perhaps with some fear, but also with hope. To one educated Norwegian immigrant, his fellow passengers had *too much* hope: "They revealed a great deal of ignorance of the states to which they were going...." he later wrote. "They seemed

to be under the impression that New York's roofs, streets, and alleys were covered with [gold and silver]." The reality was much harsher than that optimistic dream.

After 1855 immigrants arriving in New York passed through Castle Garden. The former fort-turned-opera-house had been converted into a processing center for immigrants. Here, state officials examined the health of the arrivals, recorded basic biographical information about them, and offered help finding jobs and places to stay. Each major port of entry had something similar to Castle Garden, but the U.S. government was not involved in greeting immigrants at the time. That job came after an 1875 U.S. Supreme Court decision took away from the states the duty of processing immigrants entering the country. Castle Garden closed in 1890 and in 1892 it was replaced by Ellis Island, the most famous entry point for millions of American immigrants. (See Volume 2.)

First Steps in a New Land

Once immigrants had been processed, they had to decide where to live. People without money usually stayed in the city where they arrived. Immigrants who had friends and family in the United States tended to go where those people lived. If they had no contacts, the new arrivals might head for areas where other members of their ethnic group lived, knowing they would at least find familiar languages and customs. The pattern of members of an ethnic group going to the destination of previous arrivals is called *chain migration*. One example of chain migration was when a family member—usually a husband or a son—came to America, then sent for his family after he had found a home and had enough money to support them. Chain migration also occurred on a larger scale, when whole groups of immigrants came to an area of the United States where other immigrants from their homeland had chosen to live.

Since New York was the most popular port of entry for newcomers, it became the U.S. city with the largest immigrant population. More Irish and Germans settled there than in any other city. New Orleans, as a major port of entry, had a large immigrant population, but generally, few immigrants headed for the South. The use of slaves by many Southerners meant the region offered few jobs for immigrants. In addition, immigrants from northern Europe found the South's climate too warm compared to what they were used to at home. New England, which in colonial times had attracted few immigrants, now pulled many. The region was a leading industrial center and its factories provided immigrants with jobs.

Once the immigrants reached their final destinations, they had to find jobs. Except when the American economy was slow, most immigrants could find work, although the jobs were often difficult and paid little. Aside from the immigrants involved in agriculture, most newcomers lived in or near cities where they could work in factories or in construction. Many women worked in factories as well, while others became domestic help—maids and cooks for wealthy, native-born Americans.

Since most immigrants had little money, they had to live wherever they could. Living conditions for the poor were often disgusting. Old factories or homes were sometimes converted into apartment buildings called *tenements,* where immigrants lived in crowded

rooms. Some buildings did not have real floors—just dirt or straw. Most lacked indoor plumbing, and sewage was common in the streets nearby. Such conditions led to deadly diseases such as cholera, smallpox, and malaria. To some native-born Americans, the immigrants' harsh living conditions were a reflection of their low morals, not a product of their poverty. Others, however, realized the immigrants could not control such conditions. "The poor," one doctor wrote, "can by no prudence or foresight on their part avoid the dreadful evils to which they are exposed."

Adjusting to Life in America

To cope with poverty and other difficulties of life in the United States, most immigrant groups formed mutual aid societies and other charitable and social organizations. Mutual aid societies provided insurance and other benefits to immigrants, paying for such benefits by collecting dues from the members. Benevolent societies, such as the Irish Emigrant Society, helped new arrivals find jobs or buy railroad tickets so they could join family members. The Chinese community in California was dominated by the Six Chinese Companies, powerful merchants who helped immigrants come to America, then aided them once they arrived. Family associations were also important for the Chinese—people with the same last name tended to support each other, whether they had known each other in China or not.

The sight of poor foreigners flooding the country stirred the anger and hatred of America's nativists, but some native-born citizens did respond with care and concern. The country lacked Social Security or other national public aid at the time, so charities had to step in to help the immigrants. In the 1850s some people in Boston opened a "Charity School" for children, mostly immigrants, who lived in poverty. The school provided housing, clothes, and some food, as well as education. But Charles Eliot Norton, a prominent Boston scholar, said such efforts were not enough. Help for the immigrant, he wrote, "… ought not to be left to the uncertain chances of individual capacity and private charity.…" Instead, Norton argued, the city and state governments needed to step in. Their aid, however, never matched the need, so the immigrants continued to rely on their own ethnic groups for assistance.

Immigrants needed economic help, but they needed friendship and social support as well. To provide those, ethnic groups formed clubs where members could meet, share companionship, and talk about the old country and their struggles in America. The Germans were famous for their shooting and singing clubs. Singing clubs from all over the country competed at large festivals held in German-dominated cities such as Cincinnati and St. Louis. Such clubs helped immigrants keep their cultures alive in America.

Some ethnic leaders tried to help their fellow immigrants adapt to their new lives by promoting public education and the English language. In the 1850s some people in the Scandinavian community in Wisconsin called for sending all students to American public schools so the children would learn English. But other immigrants criticized the quality of the teachers in those schools and preferred to send their children to private religious schools. Among the Germans their language was a source of pride, and German newspapers were published by the hundreds. Nevertheless, one German immigrant stressed to his countrymen "… as it concerns our means of living, we must, above and beyond all, *rely upon a knowledge of the English language.…"*

The Role of Religion

Religion and churches also played important roles for most immigrants. Through the mid–19th century some Europeans still came to America as members of religious communities, just as some early settlers had. Some Scandinavians and Poles came in that way. Within such groups a minister or other religious figure acted as the overall leader of the community.

Most immigrants, however, did not arrive with their own religious

---

Where Immigrants Arrived

The chart shows the number of immigrants who arrived at the five major U.S. seaports in the middle of the 19th century.

Year	Total	New York	Boston	Philadelphia	Baltimore	New Orleans
1846	158,000	98,000	13,000	7,000	9,000	22,000
1851	408,000	294,000	25,000	18,000	8,000	52,000
1855	230,000	161,000	17,000	7,000	6,000	20,000

SOURCE: *Natives and Strangers,* 2nd ed. (1990)

communities already in place. Members of the major religions could usually find established churches to join. Members of smaller religions had to get by on their own, as did settlers who moved west to undeveloped territories. Such people often had to rely on a lay person—someone not trained as a religious leader—to conduct religious services. Eventually, a real minister would be sent for from the old country or back East. Until a church was built, services might be held in a saloon or someone's home. Religion for most immigrants was another strong tie to their old ways, and churches provided comfort in their new home. Schools built next to churches gave immigrant children both religious education and classes in their native languages.

Religion was also important for America's Jewish immigrants and their descendants, who numbered about 150,000 at the time of the Civil War. The Jews came from different countries and were sometimes classified as two distinct groups based on their homelands: Sephardic (from Spain and Portugal) and Ashkenazic (from eastern Europe). But wherever they came from, they were united by their faith and its long history. Since the first synagogues in America dated back to the 17th century, the 19th-century arrivals could usually find religious communities when they came to the major cities of America's East Coast. But outside the East it was harder for Jews to practice their faith.

Although religion usually drew immigrants together, it could also lead to conflict. Among the Lutherans, who were usually Scandinavians or Germans, some members felt the church in America had become too liberal and Americanized. The feeling led to the formation of different *synods,* or branches, of Lutheranism. Roman Catholics also argued amongst themselves, since their church included immigrants from many different lands. By 1860 immigration had made Catholicism the largest single *denomination,* or individual form of worship, in the United States, with about 3.5 million members. The country had more Protestants but they were split up among many different denominations. Each Catholic ethnic group wanted a parish with services in its own language, and each wanted its priests to be leaders. American Judaism also had splits, as Jewish immigrants in the mid-19th century brought a new, modern form of Judaism called Reform. Its practices were more liberal than the beliefs of traditional Judaism, called Orthodox, or another branch known as Conservative.

■ Immigrants and the Civil War

As immigrants poured into America between 1840 and 1860, the issue of slavery was increasingly splitting the Union. The Southern states relied on slavery for their economy and passionately defended it. Northern states had abolished slavery, and many people in the region wanted to end it in the South as well. Politicians debated whether slavery should be expanded into the new states seeking to enter the Union. Although immigrants had their own problems adjusting to life in America, they could not escape the huge conflict that gripped the nation.

Most immigrants did not settle in the South. The reasons were usually economic: the Southern economy was based on plantation farms, worked by slaves, and did not offer the factory jobs available in the North. Many immigrants also opposed slavery for religious or moral reasons. The Irish, however, tended to be an exception. As the poorest of the white immigrants, they feared that free Southern blacks would come north and compete with them for jobs, as Northern blacks already did.

From Religion to the "Radar Range"

In 1843 the first of about 800 members of the "Community of True Inspiration" settled in Ebenezer, New York. Like other small groups of European Protestants, such believers—mostly German, but also Swiss and French—thought America offered them a place to create a perfect religious society. The community prospered and soon needed more land, preferably away from a city. The growth of nearby Buffalo, a church historian wrote, was "an injurious influence, especially on the younger members of the society."

The group's leader, Christian Metz, led the community to Iowa in 1854. Their first village there was called "Amana," a name taken from the Bible. Six other villages followed, and the Amana Society was born. All property was owned by the entire community, which included skilled craftsmen as well as farmers. The Amana Society made money in its various industries, but the group said its goal "as a religious society ... is no worldly or selfish one, but the purpose of the love of God...."

In the 1930s the society created a separate Amana Corporation, owned by the residents, that eventually manufactured household appliances. The most famous of those was the Amana "Radar Range," one of the first microwave ovens. The Amana Society no longer owns the appliance business, but it does still own its original 26,000 acres of farmland; it is the largest single farm in Iowa.

At the other extreme were the Germans, who generally opposed slavery. German Mennonites and Quakers had led the first efforts to abolish slavery back in the 17th century, and most Germans avoided living in the South. Many did settle in the slave state of Missouri because a popular German book had praised that state. When the Civil War broke out in 1861, the Germans formed militias that helped stop Missouri from leaving the Union to join the other slave states in the rebellious Confederate States of America.

The Germans were not the only immigrants to fight for the North. Most ethnic groups, including the Irish, formed their own regiments and fought bravely. The appeal for soldiers went out to everyone. In New York City a recruiting poster called for "250 able boded men! Italians, Hungarians, German, and French, patriots of all nations." Swedes, Norwegians, Jews, and free blacks also answered the call. Immigrants fought for the South as well, although in much smaller numbers. The willingness of immigrants and their descendants to fight and die for America helped end the fears of some native-born citizens that immigrants could not be good Americans.

The Civil War basically cut off the flow of new immigrants to America, ending the first major wave of U.S. immigration, since few people wanted to come during such a chaotic time. With so many men fighting and so few new people arriving, the Union faced a terrible labor crisis. In 1864 the U.S. government allowed immigrant workers to sign contracts to come to work for Northern employers. After the war the country still wanted immigrants to come. "The rapid growth and prosperity of the country," one congressional report said, "greatly depend upon foreign emigration." As America entered a new era of economic growth, immigrants were seen as a benefit to the country. But some anti-immigrant feelings remained near the surface of American public opinion.

CHAPTER 5
Conflicts in Many Colors

America's Racial Minorities

As the United States was drawing in more immigrants from abroad, it also had to address the immigrant groups already in the country. Three ethnic groups lived in a unique situation— racial prejudice by the dominant Anglo culture made their *assimilation* (adoption of American ways) particularly difficult. The "unwilling immigrants," Africans and their descendants, were the victims of slavery. The original settlers of North America, the Native Americans, were continually pushed from their lands. And Mexicans, absorbed into America after 1848, were usually treated as second-class citizens. In the years during and following the Civil War (1861–1865) each of those groups faced hard times as they tried to live in a culture—in many ways foreign to their own—that did not accept them as equals.

Life for America's Blacks

The Civil War was the worst conflict ever in the United States, splitting the country in two and resulting in hundreds of thousands of deaths. More Americans were killed than during any other war in the country's history. Although the Civil War ended slavery, it was not fought for that purpose.

In 1861 the South broke away from the Union because it believed the rights of individual states were being trampled by the federal government. The government was limiting the introduction of slavery in new states

entering the Union, and the South feared slavery would eventually be declared illegal. Many Southerners thought states had the right to decide on their own if they should allow slavery. Many also believed their region could not survive without slavery, so preserving the institution was a basic need. Others also disliked the superior tone many Northerners took when they discussed the evils of slavery. For the South the issue was cultural as well as economic.

Before Abraham Lincoln issued his Emancipation Proclamation, many black Americans, such as the one pictured below, escaped slavery by seeking the protection of the Union army. The escaped slaves were later employed by the government as laborers.

President Abraham Lincoln and his Northern supporters believed they had to stop the Southern states from leaving the Union. The United States would crumble if states could simply pull out whenever they disliked laws that were approved by the majority. Many *abolitionists*—Northerners who wanted to end all slavery—saw the war as a chance to end that cruel system once and for all. In 1863 Lincoln took that step, freeing the slaves with his Emancipation Proclamation: "I do order and declare all persons held as slaves … are, and henceforward shall be, free…." However, Lincoln's famous proclamation only freed the slaves in the states fighting the Union. Four slave states sided with the North during the war, and for them slavery did not end until after the Civil War.

The majority of America's African immigrants and their descendants had been treated as property since the mid-17th century. At the time of the Civil War the country had almost 4 million slaves and about 500,000 free blacks. Those 4.5 million blacks represented about 15 percent of America's population. Unlike other immigrants, blacks were never allowed to completely re-create their religions and cultures in their new home, although they mixed some African and Anglo elements to create an African-American culture in the United States. Southern states passed laws forbidding the education of slaves; South Carolina's law included free blacks too. Free blacks faced discrimination in the North as well as the South, although some still managed to go to school, work, and earn good livings. But the free blacks were never treated as equal citizens. In 1853 at a convention of free blacks, they pleaded their case for equal treatment. "We are Americans," they said, "and as Americans we would speak to Americans. We address you not as aliens or exiles, humbly asking to dwell among you in peace, but we address you as American citizens asserting their rights on their own native soil."

Nevertheless, in legal terms the blacks were not citizens—at least according to the Supreme Court. In 1857 in the famous *Dred Scott* case, the court ruled that slaves were property and thus could not be citizens. Free blacks were not considered U.S. citizens either, even if they had been granted citizenship in an individual state. Free blacks had also been denied one key right of citizenship—the right to vote—for decades.

Racism—the belief that one race is better than another—lay at the heart of America's slave system and feelings toward free blacks. Racism remained in place even after the Emancipation Proclamation and the end of the Civil War. A law could free a slave, but it could not change how people thought, and the racism practiced by many Americans was based on deeply held attitudes. To many slave-owning whites (and non-slave-owners as well), blacks were inferior to whites, and so they did not deserve equal legal protection or economic opportunities. Slavery, some of its defenders argued, was even better for the blacks than freedom. One Southerner wrote his defense of slavery in rhyme, praising the slave's life:

And yet the life, so unassailed by care,

So blest with moderate work, with ample fare …

Safe from harassing doubts and annual fears,

He dreads no famine in unfruitful years,

If harvest fail from inauspicious skies,

The Master's providence his food supplies….

However, few of slavery's defenders talked about the violence associated with slavery: children ripped away from their mothers, disobedient slaves whipped, runaways killed. There was deeper pain too—the emotional scars that slaves carried knowing they were not free and belonged to other human beings.

▌ After the War

The end of slavery did not end the suffering for many Southern blacks as they struggled to adapt to their new freedom and their new relationship with white Americans. The 14th Amendment to the Constitution gave blacks full citizenship and equal protection under the law. Blacks voted and ran for public office for the first time. During the era known as Reconstruction (1865–1876) Northern Republicans in Congress controlled the process for ending slavery and reestablishing governments in the defeated Southern states. Northern troops remained in the South to keep the peace during the transition from slavery to freedom for blacks. But some Southern whites resented the dominance of the North and the huge change in the status of the blacks who lived near them. Such frustrated Southerners sometimes responded with violence.

Remaining Struggles

In 1866 a group of former Confederate soldiers formed the Ku Klux Klan. What began as a social group quickly became a secret society designed to frighten blacks and their white supporters. The Klansmen raided and burned farms owned by blacks and carried out murders and kidnappings. The federal government responded with laws aimed to clamp down on terrorist groups like the Klan, and the group slowly begin to break apart. But the racist and violent attitudes that motivated many Klansmen remained. Many Southerners became alarmed at the growing role of blacks in their society. Before the 1874 election an Atlanta newspaper issued a passionate editorial calling on whites to "organize for the great struggle which seems inevitable.... We have submitted long enough to indignities, and it is time to meet brute-force with brute-force.... If the white democrats of the North are men, they will not stand idly by and see us borne down by northern radicals and half-barbarous negroes...."

A Sharecropper's Life

While traveling through Alabama in 1881 Booker T. Washington, a great black educator, described what he saw of sharecroppers' lives:

As a rule the whole family slept in one room.... At times I have eaten in cabins where they had only corn bread and black-eye peas cooked in plain water.... I found that there was no provision made in the house used for school purposes for heating the building during the winter, and consequently a fire had to be built in the yard and the teacher and pupils passed in and out of the house as they got cold or warm. With few exceptions I found the teachers in these country schools to be miserably poor in preparation for their work and poor in moral character.... I recall one day I went into a school house—or rather into an abandoned log cabin that was being used as a schoolhouse—and found five pupils who were studying a lesson from one book.... What I have said concerning the character of the schoolhouses and teachers will also apply quite accurately as a description of the church buildings and the ministers.

Widespread violence did not erupt, largely because Reconstruction ended. After the presidential election of 1876 Northern troops withdrew and

Northern politicians turned their attention away from the South. With the federal government no longer watching over them, white Southern leaders began a system of legal separation of the races. The separation, called *segregation,* forced blacks to use their own schools and hospitals and enter buildings through their own doorways—if they were allowed to enter at all. The system of laws that separated the races was called *Jim Crow,* named for a black character in a minstrel show.

Above is an 1894 photograph of Booker T. Washington.

Although blacks had escaped slavery, the new economy that replaced the plantation system was almost as bad. Many free blacks became *sharecroppers*— farmers who owned small plots of land. The sharecroppers had little or no money, so they had to borrow money or supplies to survive. Then they owed a share of their crops to the merchants who had given them the credit. Most sharecroppers never grew enough crops to pay off their debts and buy the next year's needs. Lenders did not own the sharecroppers the way masters owned slaves, but they virtually owned whatever the farmers produced and had great control over their lives.

Some Success

Jim Crow laws denied blacks their legal rights, and sharecropping kept many rural blacks poor, but some blacks were able to prosper. A black middle class developed that included shopkeepers, teachers, ministers, and skilled craftsmen. Blacks—sometimes with white financial support—set up separate colleges and universities where students could learn trades and professions. Blacks also took advantage of opportunities at mostly white colleges in the North. In the 1870s Harvard and West Point had their first black graduates, and Edward Bouchet graduated from Yale with the first Ph.D. ever awarded to a black by a U.S. university.

Of the Southern black schools, one of the most famous was the Tuskegee Institute, started by Booker T. Washington in 1881. Washington emerged as one of the great black leaders of the late 19th century. He encouraged blacks to learn practical skills rather than study the liberal arts, such as literature or philosophy. He also tried to ease tensions between whites and blacks, calling on blacks to concentrate on their economic success rather than political or social equality. The emerging black middle class generally welcomed Washington's ideas. That class was not as large or influential as the white middle class, but within the black community it offered some hope for advancement for the race as a whole.

Other blacks were not happy with the inequality they faced, and they rejected Washington's desire to accept that situation. In 1890 the Afro-American League was formed to protest the denial of legal rights to blacks; it marked one of the first times that American blacks proudly referred to their African heritage. The group's founder, T. Thomas Fortune, said the term *Afro-American* "includes every man, woman, and child in the country who is not ashamed of his race, and who insists that he shall be honorably designated as other races are...."

Six years after Fortune wrote those hopeful words, the Supreme Court squashed a legal challenge to Jim Crow laws and segregation. In *Plessey v. Ferguson* the court ruled that segregation was legal, as long as blacks had access to schools and other facilities that were the same quality as facilities for whites. "Separate but equal" was now officially the law of the land and it was eagerly practiced in the South. In reality, however, few things were ever equal for blacks. It would take more than half a century before the racist policy was reversed.

■ The Native Americans of the Plains

By the time of the Civil War the United States had taken control of Native-American lands east of the Mississippi River. The Native Americans who survived European diseases and military conquests sold their lands to whites—or were forced off them by whites. The greatest forced migration of the Native Americans came in the 1830s, when tribes of the Southeast were resettled farther west, many in the "Indian Territory" (what is now Oklahoma and part of Arkansas). For the Cherokee the forced relocation became their "Trail of Tears" as thousands died along the way.

After the Civil War Americans looked to settle the vast stretch of land between the Mississippi and the West Coast: the Great Plains. The desire for more land led to conflict with the Native Americans who lived on the plains.

Just before the Civil War silver was discovered in Colorado, drawing white settlers west. To protect its citizens, the U.S. government tried to keep the Native Americans of the region away from the Americans. In 1861 some Cheyenne, led by Chief Black Kettle, agreed to move to a reservation away from the whites. Over the next few years, however, tensions grew between the Colorado mining community and the Cheyenne, partially fueled by the racism of many of the whites toward the Native Americans.

Native Americans of the Cherokee tribes in North Carolina are the descendants of one of the few true mountaineer tribes in North America. The ones below are reviving an old tribal dance during a harvest festival.

In 1864 a group of Colorado militia, led by Colonel John Chivington, attacked a peaceful group of Cheyenne at Sand Creek. Chivington and his men held particularly rabid anti–Native-American beliefs and their assault was brutal. One American eyewitness said, "I think I saw altogether some seventy dead bodies lying there; the greater portion women and children. There may have been thirty warriors, old and young; the rest were women and children of different ages and sizes...." More than 150 Native Americans were ultimately killed during the slaughter.

After the Sand Creek Massacre, Black Kettle was reluctant to deal with the U.S. government again, but he realized that he had no choice. Part of his nation again agreed to go to a reservation. The peaceful chief was eventually killed by Colonel George Custer and his troops, who were pursuing a band of warlike Cheyenne. The Cheyenne and other Native Americans of the Great Plains and Southwest continued to resist the Americans, and the so-called Indian Wars of the 19th century continued for more than 20 years.

The coming of the whites to the plains ruined the Native Americans' way of life. American hunters wiped out the herds of buffalo on which the Plains tribes relied for food and clothing. The killing of the buffalo eventually forced many Native Americans to turn to the U.S. government for food and other basic needs.

The arrival of more U.S. troops also led many Native Americans to put down their weapons and go to the reservations. In 1871 the government stopped treating the various Native-American tribes as independent nations, and its goal was to either put all the Native Americans on reservations or wipe out those that resisted. As one government official wrote, "If they [Native Americans] stand up against the progress of civilization and industry, they must be relentlessly crushed. The westward course of population is neither to be denied nor delayed for the sake of all the [Native Americans] that ever called this country their home." Some tribes held out as long as they could, fighting the settlers and soldiers who came west.

The last major battle of the Indian Wars came in 1890 at Wounded Knee, South Dakota. It was actually another massacre, not a battle, as American troops chased a fleeing band of Sioux. From that point on the Native Americans no longer resisted the Americans, and none of the Native Americans in the United States could claim they controlled their tribal lands.

Even before Wounded Knee the U.S. government had tightened its control over the Native Americans' lives. In 1884 the government banned their religions. Three years later the Dawes Act let the government break up some reservations and sell the land to individual Native Americans and whites. Such individual ownership was foreign to the Native Americans; in their culture a whole nation owned land together. During the land sale the best reservation lands were usually sold to whites. Ninety million acres of tribal lands ended up in white hands by 1932, thanks to the Dawes Act. The law also made Native Americans eligible for U.S. citizenship for the first time, but like free blacks, Native Americans were

Clash of Cultures as Well

To most white Americans, Native Americans were no better than savages. They worshipped strange gods and did not accept the American values of private property and using nature for human gain at almost any cost. The Native Americans' culture was inferior in the eyes of Anglo society, which made it easier for whites to kill and deceive the native nations.

To Native Americans, the white people's ways were just as odd. "Certainly they are a heartless nation," one young Sioux said in the 1870s. "They have made some of their people servants—yes, slaves! ... The greatest object of their lives seems to be to acquire possessions—to be rich. They desire to possess the whole world." The Sioux found the American system of taxes even harder to accept: "... their great chief [President] compels every man to pay him for the land he lives upon and all his personal goods—even for his own existence—every year! I am sure we could not live under such a law."

second-class citizens at best. The original immigrants, whose ancestors had lived in America for thousands of years, were treated worse than many of the new arrivals just coming from Europe.

▌ The Mexicans

After the U.S. victory in the Mexican-American War (1846–1848) the country instantly had a new ethnic group in its population. Many Mexicans had already lived side by side with Anglo Americans in California, New Mexico, and Texas. But once they became U.S. residents, the Mexicans faced prejudice and discrimination in a new country they had not chosen to enter. As a result of the war, Mexico gave control of California and New Mexico (including what is now Nevada and Arizona) to America and recognized that Texas was part of the Union. (Anglo Texans had rebelled against their Mexican rulers in 1836, and then later joined the United States.)

After the war, and particularly toward the end of the 19th century, some Mexicans did enter the United States from Mexico. Like most immigrants, they provided cheap labor, although they made more money in America than they could at home. The later immigrants experienced the same prejudice the established Mexican Americans faced. At times it was even worse for the newcomers, since they were poor and usually had more of a mixed racial (Native-American or black) background. Generally, the Mexicans played an important role in helping the Anglo Americans settle the West, but their contributions were often overlooked.

Land Grabs and Mines

The Mexicans who owned land in what became part of the United States were promised they could keep it. The Treaty of Guadalupe Hildago, which had ended the Mexican-American War, guaranteed their right to those lands and let them become U.S. citizens. But as more Anglo Americans moved west, they wanted to find ways to take such lands for themselves.

In California gold was discovered the same year the Mexican-American War ended. News of the discovery was not made public until after Mexico signed the Treaty of Guadalupe Hildago—to make sure the gold-filled land would be American. People from all over the world then flocked to the region to try to strike it rich mining gold. Many of the new Mexican Americans staked claims to land that had gold, but the increasing number of Anglo miners pushed them off the land. Mexicans were sometimes lynched if they refused to give up claims.

The 1940s Native-American family shown above still practices many old customs, including spinning its own wool.

Ironically, without the Mexican miners, Anglo Americans would have had a difficult time taking the precious ore from the earth or streams. The Mexicans had been mining for hundreds of years, and they taught the Americans useful methods for extracting the most gold possible. When silver was later discovered in the West, it was again Mexican miners—many of them immigrants—who did much of the work.

For most of the 19th century Mexican immigrants moved freely across the border between their homeland and the United States, coming north to work on farms and ranches and in the mines. There was no border patrol or concept of illegal immigration (at least not for Mexicans) at the time. But once they arrived, the Mexicans could usually count on low-paying jobs and the same kind of discrimination and segregation that free blacks faced in the South. Conditions for most Mexican Americans did not improve until well into the 20th century.

CHAPTER 6
The Rush Resumes

■ Boom Times

By the end of Reconstruction (1865–1876) the U.S. economy was entering a new phase of growth. Steel mills and other factories boomed; gold and silver had been discovered in the West, and railroads spanned the entire continent. In part, Northern leaders were ready to abandon their concern for Southern blacks because they were more focused on the economic expansion. As always, the new factories and the cities growing around them created a demand for workers. Immigrants, mostly from Europe, rushed to the United States to fill that need. Another incentive to come to America was the Homestead Act of 1862. Under the law, Americans and immigrants could purchase 160 acres of land in the Midwest or on the Great Plains for just $1.25 an acre, as long as the settlers lived on the land for five years.

■ Familiar Immigrants

For the major immigrant groups of the prewar era—the Germans, Irish, and British—immigration numbers fell during the time of the Civil War (1861–1865), then immediately began to rise. German immigration hit its highest peak ever in the 1880s, when more than 1.4 million came. England set a record that decade as well, sending more than 600,000 immigrants. More of the new arrivals came with skills learned in European factories, knowing they could command higher wages in America. Before the war, when asked their occupations, almost one out of every three immigrants who responded said they were farm workers. That number fell to about 17 percent after the war. A growing number reported that they worked in industry, mining, or domestic services.

Immigration from Ireland did not match the record numbers of the famine years, but the Irish still made up a large percentage of the total number of immigrants. They continued to flock to the cities of the Northeast, and in 1870 they were the largest immigrant group in New York City, Philadelphia, and Boston. A sizable number also went to Chicago and San Francisco. The most popular West Coast destination for many immigrant groups, San Francisco had slightly more than 25,000 Irish in 1870—about one-sixth of the city's total population. During that era Irish immigration began to include more single females. They came, as single men always had, to find work; many also came to find husbands, because finding suitable mates was often difficult at home. Most of the young women worked as servants or in the textile mills of New England.

For the descendants of the prewar Irish immigrants, life was improving. Sons whose fathers might have dug ditches now could find jobs in skilled trades, such as plumbing and steamfitting (installing and repairing steam-heating systems). The Irish increasingly dominated the police and fire departments of the major cities where they settled. They also continued to play an active role in politics and in the leadership of the Roman Catholic Church.

For the Scandinavians the postwar decades marked the high point of their immigration. Both Norway and Sweden sent record numbers of immigrants in the 1880s. Following a pattern of chain migration, most Scandinavians went where the first arrivals from their homelands had already established communities—usually in the Midwest and on the Great Plains. Most Scandinavians continued to pursue farming to make their living.

The above painting depicts a settlement of immigrants in Missouri. The inscription "We left our beloved country to be happy and free in the country of the free" appeared below it.

▮ New Arrivals— The Canadians

Canada was a significant new source of immigrants after the Civil War. From 1861 to 1870 about 153,000 Canadians moved south to the United States— more than in the previous 40 years combined. That number more than doubled in the following decade.

The Canadians came from two distinct backgrounds: some had British roots, but most were French. British Canadians spoke English and tended to be Protestant, like the Anglo Americans who dominated the United States. Most

British Canadians settled in the Midwest, and they had a larger percentage of professionals such as doctors and lawyers among them than any other immigrant group. The British Canadians found it easy to *assimilate* into (adopt) American culture.

French Canadians

The situation was very different for the French Canadians. Descendants of the French founders of Quebec, they clung tightly to their language and culture. Since they were so close to their homeland, many returned or visited often, which strengthened those cultural ties and slowed their assimilation. Most settled in New England to work in textile mills or as unskilled laborers. The French Canadians were predominantly Roman Catholic, which made them targets for abuse by *nativist* (anti-immigrant) Americans. They also clashed with other Roman Catholics, particularly the Irish, as they tried to establish their own religious communities.

Most native-born Americans had an unfavorable view of French Canadians. "They care not for our institutions, civil, political, or educational," a Massachusetts official wrote in 1881. "They are a horde of industrial invaders, not a stream of stable settlers. Voting, with all that implies, they care nothing about."

Statistics show that the French Canadians did not become U.S. citizens in large numbers compared to other ethnic groups. As late as 1930, a majority had never become *naturalized* (become citizens). Without citizenship they played only a limited role in politics, even in cities where French Canadians made up a large percentage of the population. But their presence in the mills and factories of New England helped the region play a large role in America's continuing industrialization.

◼ Heading West

In the years after the Civil War more western territories opened up and then became states. Local officials in the region continued the pattern started decades before by the midwestern states—they actively recruited immigrants.

Living conditions on the plains were not easy. With few trees to turn into lumber, immigrants had to build houses out of sod bricks—packed earth and grass. Some homes were dug into the sides of hills. Others were simple lean-tos, made from a piece of wood propped up on a stick. Although plenty of land was available, most of the small plots many immigrants purchased were not suitable for farming. Rain could be scarce, leading to severe droughts, and other natural disasters struck as well. In 1874 huge swarms of grasshoppers hit the plains, destroying all the vegetation in their path. One observer wrote, "In a week grain fields, gardens, shrubs, vines, had been eaten down to the ground or the bark. Nothing could be done. You sat by and saw everything go."

Despite the risks, immigrants and native-born Americans continued to head west. Trains were often so packed with immigrants that the railroads had to add more runs. If the Great Plains were not good for some, they headed farther west to the Rocky Mountains, the Southwest, and the West Coast. Gold pulled miners to the Dakotas and Colorado, and silver attracted others to Nevada. California, with its abundance

of good land and a long coast, inspired many to move there.

◼ Nativism on the Rise

The Civil War had cooled the nativist movement, but as foreigners once again came to the United States in large numbers, nativism returned as well. It appeared in various forms, but it always had a common theme: immigrants were bad for America.

Nativism in the Workplace

The renewed nativist movement was often based on economics. Periodically, the booming American economy hit rough times and began to slow. Few new jobs were created and existing jobs were often cut back. Native-born workers did not want to compete with immigrants for jobs—especially since the immigrants accepted lower wages. Companies sometime hired immigrants in large numbers because they knew the immigrants would work for less than Americans. Sometimes the immigrant workers were hired to replace Americans out on strike who were trying to improve their wages or working conditions.

Although factory owners and other businessmen appreciated the cheap labor immigrants provided, some worried about the ideas immigrants brought with them to the workplace. The desire to form unions so workers could collectively seek better wages and working conditions was stronger in Europe than in America. *Socialism*—an economic system that said workers should one day own the mills themselves—was also developed abroad. Socialism was opposed to many of the beliefs that supported America's existing economic system, *capitalism*. Capitalists believed in free enterprise, or doing business as they wanted without the government telling them what to do. Socialists wanted the government to pass laws that forced business owners to treat workers better. Some immigrants—particularly Germans—brought socialist ideas with them to America.

American workers were becoming receptive to the idea of unions, although socialism was never broadly accepted. Many joined the Knights of Labor, which recruited members of all skill levels in many industries. The Knights also admitted women and blacks (although in segregated chapters) and fought for the eight-hour workday and the end of child labor. Many businesses resisted such changes. They wanted their employees to work long hours, and they liked using child workers because they were cheaper to hire than adults.

Although American workers might have borrowed ideas from Europe about unions, they did not welcome unskilled European laborers. In the 1880s labor groups and nativists managed to pass laws in several states that prohibited noncitizens from working on public projects, such as the building of schools and other government facilities. In Congress representatives who supported American labor complained that companies were bringing in "as so many cattle, large number of degraded, brutal … foreign serfs" to replace native-born workers.

The Haymarket Square Riot

By the 1880s the fear of European socialists was growing in America. In 1882 one magazine warned, "Our era … of happy immunity from those social diseases which are the danger and the humiliation of Europe is passing away … every year brings the conditions of American labor into close likeness to those of the Old World."

The fear of foreign radicals increased after 1886 with the Haymarket Square Riot. In May some workers held a rally in Chicago's Haymarket Square. The organizers were socialists and *anarchists*—people who believed in violently overthrowing the government. When the rally turned violent, eight anarchists were arrested—seven of them Germans. The riot led many Americans to associate all immigrants with anarchism, socialism, and violence. The incident also led to more calls to restrict immigration and to more closely control the foreigners already in the country. One newspaper called immigrants "… long-haired, wild-eyed, bad-smelling, atheistic, reckless foreign wretches," and said the country should "… crush such snakes … before they have time to bite." The Haymarket Square Riot was one of the greatest single causes for even stronger nativist attacks against immigrants.

Other Aspects of Nativism

The return of nativism was not strictly economic. Ethnic, racial, and religious prejudices also played their parts. Anti-Irish sentiments in particular were still strong. In Boston the Irish were the major immigrant group. Their growing presence upset many wealthy Bostonians who came from English families with deep roots in America. In 1887 A. Lawrence Lowell, a member of an important Boston family, voiced those feelings. He wrote that among all European immigrants, "there is, perhaps, none from which it has been more difficult to erase the foreign sentiments and qualities … than the Irish." The author focused on the old stereotype of the Irish as clannish and said that they refused to assimilate into American culture. Part of the problem was money, as the Irish still lacked economic power, and part of it was their lasting devotion to their homeland. Lowell thought such lingering loyalty was bad for the United States.

A few years later some wealthy Bostonians began the Immigration Restriction League. The league did not focus strictly on the Irish; it wanted to reduce the number of poor and unskilled immigrants from all countries because they supposedly weakened America's character. The league proposed introducing a literacy test for all immigrants.

Attacking the Chinese

During the 1870s and 1880s one immigrant group was especially targeted for nativist criticism and physical abuse: the Chinese. Like the attitudes toward European immigrants, the anti-Chinese feelings were partly economic. American workers resented the fact that the Chinese accepted lower wages or sometimes took the jobs of native-born workers who went out on strike.

But for the Chinese, racism played an even larger role in most nativist attacks. The Chinese belonged to the Asian race. Their skin color was said to be yellow, and their physical features distinguished them from whites. Many Americans took for granted that whites were superior to Asians. The racist, native-born Americans believed the Chinese were uncivilized and could not adopt the American values of democracy. One white American complained, "They never assimilate with

our people, manners, tastes, religion, or ideas."

The racism and economic conflict often led to violence across the West, when American citizens (and white immigrants) attacked the Chinese. In October 1871 riots broke out in Los Angeles. A conflict between rival Chinese gangs sparked violence that eventually led whites to attack the Chinese. Eighteen Chinese were shot or lynched. A newspaper reported that during one lynching, "The cord broke … but another was soon at hand, and he was again hoist to the beam, and there left to swing." One bystander noted that the white attackers were a mixed group, including Mexicans, a Jew, Germans, and French, as well as native-born Americans.

Another View of the Chinese

In 1879 British writer Robert Louis Stevenson traveled by train across the United States. Stevenson was famous for his novels (*Treasure Island, Dr. Jekyll and Mr. Hyde*), but he also wrote about his many travels, including his trip to the America. On the train he noticed how white Americans talked about and acted toward the Chinese.

"Of all stupid feelings," Stevenson wrote, "the sentiment of my fellow Caucasians towards our companions in the Chinese car was the most stupid and the worst." He described how the Americans made a choking noise whenever they saw a Chinese person, and they considered the Chinese dirty, stupid, and cruel. But Stevenson had a different opinion. "For my own part, I could not look but with wonder and respect on the Chinese. Their forefathers watched the stars before mine had begun to keep pigs. Gunpowder and printing, which the other day we imitated … were theirs in long-past antiquity." They had "philosophy so wise, that our best philosophers find things therein to wonder at." After watching how the Americans treated the Chinese—and Native Americans as well—Stevenson wrote, "I was ashamed for the thing we call civilization."

New Immigration Laws

Racist thinking was reflected in U.S. laws, which said only white people could become naturalized citizens.

After the Civil War the 14th Amendment to the Constitution made any person born in the country a citizen, and the rule applied to Chinese children as well, but their parents were still denied naturalized citizenship. Some nativists wanted even more legal action against the Chinese. Californians led the call for a law to keep additional Chinese from entering the country, and in 1882 Congress passed the Chinese Exclusion Act. The act was the first immigration law to forbid the entry of a particular ethnic group. With few exceptions Chinese immigration ended for 60 years.

Also in 1882 Congress passed the first comprehensive national immigration act, which placed a tax of 50 cents on each person entering the country. The law also excluded "convicts, lunatics, idiots, and persons likely to become a public charge." Future immigration laws continued to place restrictions on who could enter America, but millions of immigrants still streamed into the country for decades to come.

CHAPTER 7
The "New" Immigrant

◼ A Mixed Response to Immigrants

The debate over immigration continued as the United States entered the 1890s. Some scholars were more vocal in defending immigration as something positive for the country. One economist pointed out that immigrants eagerly accepted difficult, low-paying jobs that few native-born Americans wanted. Another scholar admired the courage the immigrants showed in leaving their homelands and coming to America. He wrote, "So long as they will come, so long as we need them—a question which cannot possibly arise for discussion until our population has multiplied ten- or twenty-fold—we cannot afford, either in fairness or in humanity, to erect a single barrier against the flow of this tide of men." Of course, women were also a part of the tide and played an important role in the workplace.

The American economy, however, suffered one of its worst downturns of the century in 1893. There were several factors that led up to the economic problems, including disastrous weather in previous years that destroyed crops and cattle, a decline in foreign trade due to high tariffs, and a drop in the gold reserves held by the U.S. Treasury that caused investors to panic and businesses to fail. The economic troubles led to increased calls for limiting immigration. New laws were not really necessary, since fewer immigrants chose to come when times were so tough. Immigration for the decade from 1891 to 1900 dropped to about 3.7 million after passing 5 million in the previous

decade. Still, *nativist* (anti–immigrant) sentiments to restrict immigration were strong and they were partly stirred by changes in the types of immigrants reaching America.

From 1881 to 1890 about 80 percent of immigrants still came from the

Immigrants in the Cities

The chart below shows the numbers of various foreign-born residents in selected U.S. cities in 1890.

New York

Total Population	1,515,000
Germans	211,000
Irish	190,000
Russians	49,000
Austro-Hungarians	48,000
Italians	40,000
Other	94,000

Chicago

Total Population	1,100,000
Germans	161,000
Irish	70,000
Swedes	43,000
Austro-Hungarians	33,000
Canadians	24,000
Other	96,000

Milwaukee

Total Population	204,000
Germans	55,000
Polish	9,000
Other	16,000

Minneapolis

Total Population	165,000
Swedes	19,000
Norwegians	13,000
Germans	8,000
Canadians	8,000
Other	13,000

SOURCE: *A Distant Magnet* (1971)

traditional sources: Ireland, Great Britain, Germany, and Scandinavia. But for the first time an increasing number were coming from southern and eastern Europe. That trend continued in the 1890s, as immigrants from those regions made up more than half of all the new arrivals from Europe.

Above is a 1905 photograph of the Registry Building on Ellis Island.

The causes of the increased immigration from those regions were familiar. Most of the newcomers were escaping poverty and a lack of jobs. Many people in eastern Europe also resented foreign control of their homelands. Germany, Russia, and the Austro-Hungarian Empire dominated lands filled with minority ethnic groups. The governments of those countries sometimes denied such minorities full legal rights. Russian Jews had a specific problem: they faced intense anti-Semitism (hostility toward or discrimination against Jews). The Russian government limited their educational opportunities and forced them to serve long terms in the military. The government also encouraged its

citizens to carry out deadly attacks on Jews, called *pogroms.*

■ Arrivals from Southern and Eastern Europe

After 1892 many southern and eastern European immigrants passed through a new checkpoint when they reached New York: Ellis Island. The U.S. government had taken full control of inspecting immigrants when they arrived in America, and Ellis Island was the most famous of its processing stations. Passengers who traveled in steerage usually took ferries from the New York docks to the island. At Ellis Island they were examined for diseases and government inspectors made sure they could be allowed into the country under existing laws. Most immigrants quickly passed through the inspections and continued on their way to New York City or beyond. Others, however, were detained because of illness or were sent back to their homelands. (See Volume 2.) One Russian Jewish woman saw her grandmother sent back to Russia. "They found my grandmother had a black nail," the woman later said. "She raised us, all the years, with that hand and with that nail. There was nothing wrong with it.… They sent her back.… So we never saw her again. I'm still crying over it."

Over time Americans sensed that a greater number of the country's newcomers were culturally and ethnically different from the Germans, Irish, and Scandinavians who had come before in such great numbers. In 1911 a report from a government study that had begun four years earlier lumped together the southern and eastern Europeans as "new" immigrants. The recent immigrants did have some things in common: most were poor and a majority settled in the cities of the Northeast. But such ethnic groups also had many differences, and sometimes even within a group, not all members shared the same religion or culture.

■ The Italians

The largest ethnic group of all the new immigrant groups was the Italians. For 40 years starting in 1881, more than 4 million Italians came to America. Many of those immigrants did not stay in America, but the millions who did spread out all over the country.

Like Germany, the modern nation of Italy did not emerge until the last half of the 19th century, and the Italians had distinct regional differences. They spoke many dialects and were likely to associate mostly with people from their own region. The regional identity Italians brought with them was sometimes even more local, extending to just a village. It was not uncommon for people from one village in Italy to settle in the same town or neighborhood in America. Most of the immigrants also put a strong emphasis on family loyalty.

The first Italians to reach the United States tended to come from northern Italy. The bulk of the later arrivals came from the south and the island of Sicily, where poverty was greater than in the north. Northern Italians were more likely to go into farming than their southern counterparts; the southerners worked more often in unskilled jobs, much as the Irish had done decades before. Many of the "new" Italian immigrants of the late 19th century were single males who came to the United States to work for a few years, then returned to Italy. Such immigrants,

who do not intend to stay in the United States, are sometimes called *sojourners*. Some Italians stayed in America and later sent for their families. Others went back and forth between the two countries a number of times. Some immigrants did come as families planning to stay in America.

In the Work Force

Coming with few skills and little or no education, many Italians turned to help from other Italians already established in America. Italian labor bosses hired new immigrants to work in construction gangs and in mines and factories. The bosses were called *padrones,* and the padrone system helped the immigrants adjust to life in their new home. Other ethnic groups, such as the Greeks and Syrians, developed similar systems.

However, the padrone system also led to abuse. The bosses knew they could take advantage of the newcomers, since the immigrants were trusting and had few other options to find work. The recent arrivals also rarely spoke English and were reluctant to complain to the police or local officials if they were treated badly. In 1885 the U.S. government tried to weaken the padrone system by ending contract labor; labor bosses could no longer recruit workers abroad and sign them to contracts before they came to the United States. But the padrone system endured and so did its hardships. In 1893 one Italian American described some of the worst aspects of the system:

> The brutality of the contractors toward their subjects baffles description.... He often keeps guards armed with Winchester rifles to prevent men from running away. His power has the

essential characteristics of a government. He fines his men and beats and punishes them for any attempted resistance to his self-constituted authority.

California Calls

For Italians who did not stay in the cities of the Northeast, California was a popular destination. Its weather was similar to the warm climate of southern Italy, and some of its valleys provided perfect conditions for growing grapes used to make wine. Although the first vineyards were already established before the Italians came, the Italians quickly became major California winemakers.

In 1881 the Italian-Swiss Agricultural Colony—a winemaking colony—was founded by an Italian immigrant, Andrea Sbarbaro, in the Russian River Valley. A group of winemakers pooled their money and bought about 1,500 acres that were once a sheep ranch. They cleared the land and introduced European grapes to the California soil. Within 20 years, according to Sbarbaro, the colony ran a thriving business and had "built a settlement for 100 families, erected a schoolhouse where many children, most of them born on the premises, already attend, have a railroad station, post office, and telephone, and have laid the foundation for a new city." In 1897 the colony had built what may have been the world's largest wine tank of the era. The tank held 500,000 gallons, and when it was finished 200 people celebrated with a party held inside the huge cement structure.

Other Italian winemakers were successful throughout California and Italian farmers grew many other crops besides grapes. Sbarbaro, however, moved on to another field. In 1899 he founded the Italian-American Bank of San Francisco

Not all Italians dealt with the padrone system. Many found honest—if still demanding and low-paying—work. Others were able to succeed on a larger scale. In the 1880s Italian farmers and winemakers began to settle in California, helping to establish America's wine industry. (See "California Calls" sidebar.) Many others started small shops, such as grocery stores, and became successful merchants.

Reaction to the Italians

Americans had mixed reactions to the Italians entering the country. Even native-born citizens who saw positive qualities in the Italians stereotyped the entire ethnic group. In 1906 one American educator called them "hot-blooded" and "ignorant" yet also said they were "patient" and "faithful." "They are honest," he continued, "saving, industrious, temperate and so exceptionally moral ... they are the very flower of [Italy's] peasantry."

Such glowing words, however, were not as common as the attacks many Americans made on the Italians' character—especially the southern Italians. Coming in large numbers and often living in poverty, Italians did have some criminals in their communities, just as every other ethnic group did—including the native-born white Americans. But some people were quick to see all Italians as violent and lawless. In 1890 an American lawyer wrote, "The knife with which he cuts his bread he also uses to lop off another 'dago's' finger or ear.... He is quite as familiar with the sight of human blood as he is with the food he eats."

The existence of crime gangs in Italy also carried over to the United States. To many Americans, Italian organized crime gangs were destroying the country. Certainly, a small number of Italians belonged to such groups as the Mafia and the Camorra—crime gangs with roots in Italy. But some newspapers also wrote feverishly about the Black Hand gang, supposedly notorious for murder and theft. In reality the gang did not exist; it was the creation of a New York City reporter. Some Italian-American criminals then adopted the name and acted like they were a gang, just so they could force bribes out of gullible victims.

Many Americans were ready to believe the worst about Italians. Like many southern European immigrants, they seemed to stand out from other immigrants and native-born Americans because of their dark hair and complexions. The Italians became a symbol for everything wrong with the "new" immigrant.

■ Jews from Russia and Elsewhere

The pogroms and general anti-Semitism in Russia drove many Jews to come to America. Although living under Russian control, many of the Jews actually came from areas now outside of Russia: Poland, Lithuania, Belarus. Others came from Austria-Hungary. But the Russian Jews were the most typical Jewish immigrants to America from 1890 into the early 20th century. About 2 million Jews from all countries arrived during that period; unlike the Italians, few left once they settled in America.

The Jews sometimes spoke Russian (or the native tongue of their former homeland) or Hebrew, but most spoke Yiddish, a language that mixes elements of a German dialect and Hebrew. By speaking Yiddish the new Jewish arrivals set themselves apart from the German Jews who had come to America in the mid-19th century. The earlier Jewish immigrants now had thoroughly *assimilated* (adapted American ways), and they considered Yiddish—which they did not speak— less dignified than German or Hebrew. The language difference was just one issue that created tension between the German and eastern European Jews. The German Jews did not want to be associated with the large number of poor newcomers that seemed so alien to many native-born Americans. Gradually, however, the German Jews set up charitable organizations to aid the new Jews and speed their assimilation into American life.

Life in the City

Like most immigrants, the Jews arrived poor, although many of them had been merchants or had worked at skilled trades in their homelands. Although they came mostly from rural areas, they tended to settle in the cities of the Northeast—particularly New York. Historian Moses Rischin called New York "the promised city" for Jews. In New York the Jews took jobs in the cigar- and garment-making trades and soon began to dominate those industries. Others worked independently as tailors, bakers, butchers, or shopkeepers. Many Jews sold goods from pushcarts, and the Lower East Side, which became a popular Jewish neighborhood, was often filled with the cries of peddlers selling their wares.

Many immigrants settled in large cities throughout the United States, such as New York City—shown here in a 1925 street scene.

The Jews in New York lived in *tenements*—crowded apartment buildings common throughout the city—as many immigrants had before them. Tenements, one reporter wrote, were often "prison-like structures of brick, with narrow doors and windows.... In the hot summer months ... fire escape balconies are used as sleeping rooms by the poor wretches who are fortunate enough to have windows opening upon them." Poverty forced the Jews to live in such unpleasant surroundings, and families often had to take in lodgers to help pay for their rent.

Becoming an American

New York may have been the "promised city" for Jews, but to Mary Antin, all of America was the "promised land." That was also the title of her autobiography, written in 1911 and first published in the *Atlantic Monthly* magazine. Antin was a Russian Jew who came to the United States in 1894 when she was 13. She settled with her family in Boston, although later she moved to New York.

The Promised Land tells how Antin became *assimilated* into (adapted) American culture and developed a love for her new home. For her, as for many immigrants, the process started in school. "I could not pronounce the name of George Washington without pause," she wrote. "As I read about the noble boy who would not tell a lie to save himself from punishment, I was for the first time truly repentant of my sins ... he and I were Fellow Citizens.... It thrilled me to realize what sudden greatness had fallen on me; and at the same time, it sobered me, as with a sense of responsibility. I strove to conduct myself as befitted a Fellow Citizen.... And when we stood up to sing "America," I shouted the words with all my might. I was in very earnest proclaiming to the world my love for my new-found country."

The Jews' homes often doubled as their workplaces. Some garment makers sewed in their homes. One observer described walking through the Lower East Side and hearing "the whir of a thousand sewing machines, worked at high pressure from earliest dawn till mind and muscle give out together.... It is not unusual to find a dozen persons—men, women, and children— at work in a single room."

The Jews worked hard so they could eventually move out of the tenements and into better housing. Most Jewish parents wanted to give their children the education and opportunities they lacked living under Russian domination. By the second and third generations, Jewish children were taking advantage of education to become doctors, lawyers, and other professionals. The Russian Jews also began to play a prominent role in labor organizations, trying to improve working conditions for themselves and other immigrant workers.

Reaction to the Jews

Some Americans saw the hard-working, educated Russian Jews as assets. In 1893 one journalist praised them for their political intelligence and business skills. "They have made possible the establishment of new industries. For example, twenty years ago nine-tenths of all the cloaks used in this country were imported, but nine-tenths have been made here since the beginning of the large immigration of Russian Jews.... They and their descendants are destined to become a permanent factor in our national life."

But like the Italians, Jews were more likely to meet hostility than receive a warm welcome. Jews were seen as another large element in the wave of new, less desirable immigrants entering the United States. The Jews had another disadvantage: the traditional anti-Semitism they faced in Europe and— to a lesser extent—in America. Anti-Semitism had been increasing in America since the 1870s. At that time some German Jews began to achieve economic success, which caused resentment among some Americans.

The Jews also practiced a non-Christian religion and had been branded with many negative stereotypes by Europeans since the Middle Ages. The rising number of eastern European Jewish immigrants after 1890 increased the native-born Americans' dislike of all Jews.

In 1896 growing anti-Semitism led to wild comments about Jews in general and American Jews in particular. A Protestant minister warned, "The time is coming when the Jews will rule the world.... The largest commercial interests in New York are already in their hand. The day is fast approaching when an anti-Christ will rise among the Jews who will devastate the nations of Europe...."

If the Jews were not feared for their supposed business domination, they were considered socially inferior. Private clubs and schools refused to admit them, and businesses limited how many Jews they hired and how far the Jews advanced. As early as 1881, New York officials tried to fight discrimination with laws. The city's civil rights code prohibited using religious beliefs as grounds for discrimination. But prejudicial attitudes against the Jews remained.

■ The Poles and Other Slavs

By one estimate the Poles were the third-largest ethnic group to enter the United States during the period of "new" immigration, but figures are not precise. During the peak years of the era, from 1899 to 1919, Poles were classified as Austro-Hungarians, Russians, and Germans, since those countries controlled the lands that once comprised an independent Polish nation. People living in what had been Poland included ethnic Germans, Lithuanians, Jews, and Poles; the following section deals with the ethnic Poles. In the 1910 Census about 950,000 people said they spoke Polish as their first language and were born abroad. Another 1.7 million people were second-generation Polish Americans.

The Poles who came to the United States before the end of the 19th century were mostly upper-class citizens. The new Polish immigrants, however, were mostly poor and unskilled. When they arrived in America, they took jobs in eastern coal mines and steel mills or flocked to the factories of the Midwest. Chicago eventually developed the largest Polish community in the country, with an estimated 400,000 Polish Americans living there by 1920.

The Poles were joined by other Slavs—a broad term for the peoples of eastern Europe who once shared a common language. Many Americans referred to the Slavs collectively as "Hungarians," since they came from what was then the Austro-Hungarian Empire. Ethnic Hungarians, however, are not Slavs and are called Magyars.

The major Slavic immigrant groups that came to the United States included non-Jewish Russians, Czechs, Slovaks, Ukrainians, Bulgarians, Serbs, Croats, and Slovenes. Although there are some similarities among the different Slavic languages, the various ethnic groups that immigrated had many cultural differences. Religiously, some were Roman Catholics, such as the Poles, Slovaks, and Czechs. Others followed different versions of the Eastern Orthodox religion, which was once united with Roman Catholicism but split off from it hundreds of years ago. The Roman Catholic Slavs typically used the Latin alphabet, which is used for English as well. Most Orthodox Slavs used the Cyrillic alphabet, which is based on the Greek alphabet and was developed about a thousand years ago.

A Killing in Georgia

In the South blacks accused of a crime were sometimes taken by white mobs and lynched—or hung—without a trial. In one famous lynching, however, a Jewish American died in that gruesome way. The killing was one of the worst examples of American anti-Semitism (hostility toward or discrimination against Jews) ever.

In the early 1900s Leo Frank was a college educated Northerner who moved to Georgia. He became the manager and part-owner of a pencil factory. When a young girl who worked at the factory was found dead in 1915, Frank was immediately a suspect. He was convicted of the murder and sentenced to death even though there was no evidence against him.

Wealthy Northern Jews and some Georgia ministers began a campaign to give Frank a new trial, and the governor eventually changed his sentence to life imprisonment. In the meantime, local anti-Semites stirred up anger toward Frank and all Jews. One of them, Tom Watson, said the Jews arriving from Europe were "scum and dregs."

While he was in prison, Frank was beaten up by both white and black prisoners. Then on August 16, 1915, an angry mob from Marietta, the hometown of the murdered girl, stormed the prison hospital. They grabbed Frank and took him 175 miles to Marietta, where they lynched him. The Frank case remains one of the most famous acts of violent anti-Semitism in American history.

Work and Social Life

Like the Italians, many Slavs planned on working in America for only a few years and then returning home. The Czechs were one exception: they tended to come as families and set down permanent roots. They had started coming to America and establishing ethnic settlements before the Civil War (1861–1865), as had the Poles. Many Czechs also went to existing cities—particularly Chicago. Some were farmers, while others worked in lumbering. Later Czech immigrants,

along with Poles and other Slavs, ended up in factories.

At times the different Slavic groups looked to settle in their own individual communities, but they were also known to share the same neighborhoods. In 1901 a New York City social worker studied a Slavic neighborhood just across the Hudson River in Jersey City, New Jersey. She found Poles, Russians, and some "Hungarians" (likely Slovaks) living together. Not surprisingly, the immigrants settled near the factories where they worked. They lived in crowded tenements—the only housing they could afford. Like other immigrants, the Slavs needed better housing and education for their children to improve their lives in the United States.

Ethnic Identity

Since the Slavs came from lands controlled by other nations, for the most part many did not have any sense of national or ethnic identity. Like other immigrants, such as the Italians, they were more apt to feel strong ties to their family and village than to a larger ethnic group. One immigrant living in Brooklyn said, "Us Slovaks didn't know we were Slovaks until we came to America and they told us!"

The Poles, however, were one Slavic group that arrived with a strong sense of national identity. They had developed it during the years when Poland was an independent nation. The Poles were also fiercely devoted to their Roman Catholic religion—more so than many other Catholic immigrants in America. Like other Catholics who came after the Irish, the Poles often clashed with the Catholic Church's largely Irish-American leadership. The Poles resented any attempt to limit the use of their native language or deny them their rights. Their language, religion, and national pride were all closely bound together.

The Poles and the other Slavs faced a familiar balancing act: trying to keep their native languages and traditions while facing pressure to assimilate into American culture. Although the Slavs as a group were seldom the victims of the strong nativist attacks that Italians and Jews experienced, they were still likely to be lumped in as members of the undesirable "new" immigrants.

▌ Other Immigrants from Europe and Beyond

In addition to the Italians, a number of other immigrants came from the lands that surround the Mediterranean Sea. Some of those people were European, such as the Portuguese and Greeks. Others lived in the Middle East, such as the Syrians and other Arabs. Together, the Mediterranean peoples added a few million more immigrants to the mix of new immigrants coming to America.

Greeks

Up until 1900 Greek immigration was fairly low, but in the first two decades of the 20th century more than 350,000 Greeks came to the United States. Many came as sojourners and planned to return home once they earned money; about half ultimately returned. Some Greeks came to avoid high taxes or military duty at home. Other Greeks who lived in areas controlled by the Ottoman Empire came to escape prejudice by the ruling Turks. The Ottoman Empire dominated large portions of the Middle East and southeastern Europe (the Balkans)

at the time, and many immigrants from a variety of ethnic groups came to America from those lands.

Like other immigrants of the era, the Greeks settled mostly in cities across the country. They worked in factories but also held such wide-ranging jobs as sheepherders and railroad crewmen. The Greeks worked hard to improve their economic conditions. For many of them owning their own business was the ultimate goal. In the late 19th and early 20th centuries Greeks often peddled goods from pushcarts, saving money to open their own stores. In many cities Greeks began to dominate the floral industry, running retail flower shops. Greeks were also prominent in the candy business. In 1904 a Greek newspaper in Chicago noted that "practically every busy corner in Chicago is occupied by a Greek candy store." Greeks often owned restaurants as well.

The Greeks belonged to the Greek Orthodox Church, and religion played an important role in their lives. In the 1890s and early 1900s Greeks built churches in growing numbers; before then, there was just one Greek Orthodox church in the United States. Along with the churches, they built schools so their children could learn the Greek language.

Portuguese

The Portuguese had a rich heritage of sailing and fishing in their homeland, and many immigrants continued that tradition in the United States. More than 100,000 came between 1881 and 1910, and many settled along the Atlantic Coast of New England. New Bedford, Massachusetts, became a largely Portuguese community. Others went in numbers to California and turned to agriculture.

A Portuguese community also developed in Hawaii, where the first Portuguese arrived in 1878. By the early 20th century the plantation owners of the islands were actively recruiting Portuguese farm workers to reduce the need for Asian workers. After three shiploads of Portuguese (and some Spanish) workers arrived in 1911, a government official noted that "... these immigrants seem to be satisfactory and appear generally contented with conditions as they find them in Hawaii." By that time, earlier Portuguese immigrants had introduced to Hawaii a tiny four-stringed instrument from their homeland called a *machete*. The instrument is known today as the *ukulele* and is closely associated with Hawaiian culture.

Immigrants often started their own businesses by peddling their wares on the streets. Stores were opened as these businesses prospered.

Syrians

Identifying exactly who was a Syrian immigrant and how many came to America is not easy. The modern country of Syria did not exist at the turn of the 19th century, and many people who called themselves Lebanese were labeled as Syrians by the U.S. government. Another complication is that the Middle Eastern land where Syrians and Lebanese lived was part of the Ottoman Empire. Therefore, they traveled to the United States on Turkish passports and were sometimes recorded as Turkish immigrants. But the Syrians, Lebanese, and other Arabs of the area were not ethnically Turkish and many were Christians. The Turks were Muslims, and their discrimination against the Christians was one reason why many non-Muslim Syrians and Lebanese chose to emigrate.

Syrian immigration was never large: an estimated 70,000 lived in America in 1907. Many were Roman Catholics, while others belonged to the Greek Orthodox Church or other Christian religions. A tiny minority of Syrians and other Arab immigrants of the time were Muslims; the entire United States had just two or three *mosques* (Muslim houses of worship) before the 1930s.

Many Syrians settled in the Northeast, and like most ethnic groups, established communities with other immigrants from their homeland. In some cases individuals or single families set out on their own and lived among native-born Americans or immigrants from other countries. Like the Greeks, the Syrians tended to start their own businesses, selling goods from pushcarts or opening small shops. A few moved to the plains states to farm.

Since the Syrians came in small numbers, they were not usually targets for anti-immigrant attacks, but because they came from Arab lands, they were for a time considered nonwhite and denied American citizenship—even if they had light hair and blue eyes. It took a number of court rulings for some Syrian immigrants to become *naturalized* Americans (citizens).

Armenians

The Armenians were not a Mediterranean people, as the Syrians were, but they were similar in other ways. Their country was also under Turkish control, and they were a Christian minority in a Muslim land—however, the Armenians were singled out by the Turks for especially cruel treatment.

Starting in the 1890s the Turks began a campaign to drive the Armenians from their homeland. Because of violent attacks, Armenians began fleeing to the United States. About 50,000 managed to come before World War I (1914–1918). The worst Turkish violence against the Armenians came during the war, when up to one million were slaughtered. One Armenian American, a survivor of the violence, recounted her experience: "They all die, 25 people in my family die. You can't walk, they kill you. You walk, they kill you. They did not care who they kill. My husband … he saw his mother's head cut off."

The Armenians traveled under Turkish and sometimes Russian passports, so the numbers for their immigration are not accurate. Unlike many of the immigrants of the time from eastern and southern Europe, a number of Armenians were literate and skilled. In their homeland many had been artisans, merchants, or bankers, and they went into business in America, often importing and selling Oriental rugs. Armenians also dominated parts of the printing industry. In agriculture a large farming community developed around Fresno, California, and Armenians there eventually bought vineyards and ranches.

Not everything was peaceful for the Armenians in their new home. Some Californians labeled them "undesirable" immigrants and passed laws preventing them from voting or owning land. Like the Syrians, the Armenians also faced legal battles to become naturalized citizens.

■ New Asian Immigrants— the Japanese

After 1882 legal Chinese immigration to the United States ended, but just a few years later a new Asian people began to come in increasing numbers: the Japanese. Immigration from Japan reached its peak between 1901 and 1910, when more than 129,000 came to America. A large community also developed in the Hawaiian Islands, which became a U.S. territory in 1898. The Japanese who came to the mainland stayed almost exclusively on the West Coast, and California was typically their home.

Like the Chinese, the Japanese took jobs in mines. They also worked as loggers and in plants where food was canned. Most Japanese, however, turned to agriculture, and they quickly became efficient and hard-working farmers. Their success stirred up jealousy among native-born farmers who faced stiff competition from the new immigrants. That jealousy created anger and suspicion similar to what the Chinese had experienced decades before.

Part of the prejudice and discrimination against the Japanese was racial, since they were another "yellow" people. Many were not Christians—they practiced Buddhism or Shintoism, a native Japanese religion. Many Americans developed stereotypes about them, questioning their morals and their loyalty. California nativists said the Japanese lacked the values that would make them good Americans. Of course, first-generation Japanese could not become citizens even if they wanted to; the law that prohibited nonwhite immigrants from becoming naturalized prevented that. One newspaper called the Japanese a "Yellow Peril" that was crowding out the whites of California.

Many Californians pushed for restricting Japanese immigration just as they had done with the Chinese. They also tried to pass laws that made life difficult for the immigrants already in their state. In 1905 San Francisco officials put Japanese children into segregated schools. The incident triggered a protest from the government of Japan and angered President Theodore Roosevelt, who wanted good foreign relations with Japan. He stepped in to have the order reversed, then negotiated the "Gentlemen's Agreement" with Japan. The Japanese government agreed to voluntarily end the immigration of unskilled workers.

The Japanese were not the typical "new" immigrants of the late 19th and early 20th centuries. Their numbers were too small outside of California to make much of a national impact. But they shared many experiences with the other immigrants of the era. Members of each ethnic group found some success in America, compared to their old lives, while others returned to their homelands. Most who stayed faced hard work and poverty, at least for a time.

CHAPTER 8
Helping Hands and Threatening Fists

◼ The Uncertainty Continues

With the rise of immigration after 1890 and the changing nature of the immigrants, Americans responded in different ways to the newcomers. Some wanted to help immigrants adapt to life in the United States. Their aid was sometimes social and economic; other times it came as efforts to ease the immigrants' *assimilation* (adoption of American ways). Even those good intentions, however, were sometimes tainted by anti-immigrant prejudices.

On the other hand some Americans reacted with increased *nativism* (anti-immigrant feelings) and examples of prejudice against certain ethnic groups, or against all new immigrants in general. (See Chapter 7.) The prejudice was motivated sometimes by economic concerns, sometimes by racism, and often by a combination of the two. The nativist impulse continued to rise up to and after World War I (1914–1918).

◼ Positive Reactions to Immigrants

During the 19th century the growth of industries in Europe and the United States had drawn millions of people off farms and into cities looking for jobs. The movement of people from rural areas to cities is called *urbanization*. The process was frightening to some Americans: urbanization created large, crowded cities that were often the homes of poverty, crime, and disease. Because America's growing cities contained so many immigrants, especially after the 1880s, the

immigrants were often associated with—or blamed for—such urban problems. In reality the social and economic problems of the cities were largely beyond the immigrants' control. The immigrants also had additional difficulties to overcome compared to native-born city dwellers. The newcomers had to struggle with a foreign language and culture, as well as the insecurity that can arise when people are cut off from their traditional lifestyle.

In the 1880s some Americans began to look for ways to help solve the urban problems of the day and ease immigrants into their new home. Such social reformers borrowed an idea developed in England: sending young, college educated people to settle in poor urban areas. The students then helped the residents improve their lives and learned more about the conditions the people faced. The social workers lived in special homes, called *settlement houses*. The settlement houses, which were community centers for immigrants, soon sprang up in many cities and larger towns; by 1900 the country had more than 100 of them. The most famous and influential settlement house was run by a woman named Jane Addams.

Hull House and the Settlement House Movement

Chicago in 1890 rivaled New York as the most ethnically diverse city in the country. More than 400,000 first-generation immigrants of various ethnic backgrounds lived in the "Windy City"; combined with their second-generation descendants, such immigrants outnumbered native-born Americans. The census that year showed that Chicago had Germans, Irish, Poles, Jews, Italians, Bohemians (Czechs), Russians, French, Greeks, Swedes, Norwegians, Scots, English, various Asians, Hungarians, Romanians, Portuguese, Canadians, and small numbers of other groups. The year before those figures had been collected, Jane Addams had founded the city's first settlement house, called Hull House.

Above is a photograph of Jane Addams in her early days at Hull House.

Addams took over an old mansion on Chicago's West Side and made it a social and education center for the city's poor. Hull House gave immigrants a place to come for aid in adjusting to life in their new homeland. "The Settlement," Addams wrote, "is valuable as an information and interpretation bureau. It constantly acts between various institutions of the city and the people for whose benefit these institutions were erected.... Another function of the Settlement to its neighborhood resembles that of the big brother whose mere presence on the

playground protects the little ones from bullies."

Hull House and other settlement houses taught immigrants English, provided day care and kindergartens for the children of working mothers, donated food and medicine to unemployed workers and their families, and did whatever else they could to help immigrants in need. Addams and others like her also helped immigrants keep their cultural roots while becoming assimilated, allowing various immigrant groups to use the houses as meeting places and sponsoring ethnic celebrations. The social workers did not think being a good American and retaining ethnic roots were contradictory, as many nativists did.

The settlement house workers also took on bigger issues, such as ending child labor, improving working conditions for factory workers, and stopping political corruption in city governments. Those efforts were part of a larger reform movement in America called Progressivism. Progressivism marked the first large reform movement of the industrial era. The Progressive movement was also one of the few times in the 19th century that the Anglo, Protestant culture reached out to help immigrants on a large scale.

Economic Benefits

In the early 20th century the U.S. economy was strong again after the downturn of the 1890s. Once again, many Americans praised the immigrants' main contribution to their new land: their labor. The first generation of immigrants had assimilated, sent their children to school, and moved into better-paying, middle-class jobs. The country needed more people to take the heavy labor and factory jobs that had made America the most industrialized nation in the world. People who saw that need realized immigrants were crucial to the country's continued growth. A Pittsburgh YMCA worker observed, "… as a whole, [immigrants] bring with them physical and cultural resources which the English-speaking community fails to elicit or thoughtlessly wastes.…"

In 1897 President Grover Cleveland saw the immigrants' positive impact as well. Congress that year passed a bill to introduce a literacy test for newcomers, but Cleveland vetoed the bill. He said that America had a tradition of welcoming people from other lands, and that the country's economic growth came in large part by assimilating "millions of sturdy and patriotic adopted citizens.…"

■ Turning Immigrants into Americans

Despite the encouragement some Americans gave immigrants, the newcomers still had difficulties entering into the dominant culture. Americans sometimes questioned the abilities of southern and eastern Europeans to adopt so-called American values. (Nativists had voiced a similar fear in the past about other ethnic groups.) Other native-born citizens disagreed over the best ways to help the immigrants assimilate. The new immigrants, like immigrants before them, often felt a pull within themselves: they wanted to be good Americans but did not want to cast away all the benefits of their old cultures and traditions. The great increase in immigration at the turn of the 19th century made assimilation a heated issue

during the first two decades of the 20th century—more so than it had been in the past.

The Melting Pot?

U.S. citizens and outside observers alike had sometimes described the United States as a place where people of many lands came together to form a new social group, called Americans. The people did not necessarily share the same ethnic backgrounds or religions— at least, not at first—but they did share a faith in democracy and personal freedom. The goal of assimilation was to shape the immigrant into that new kind of person. The country's motto seemed to sum up the idea: *E pluribus unum,* Latin for "Out of many, one."

In 1908 Israel Zangwill, an English playwright of Russian-Jewish descent, produced a play called *The Melting-Pot.* The work illustrated the ideal of assimilation, of combining many ethnic groups into the unique American culture. At one point, the play's hero says, "… Celt and Latin, Slav and Teuton, Greek and Syrian, black and yellow.… Here shall they all unite to build the Republic of Man and Kingdom of God." After Zangwill's play, many Americans used the term "melting pot" to describe their country—a country where people from many different racial, ethnic, and religious backgrounds melted, or blended, together to form a united group.

Not long after the melting pot idea gained favor, some scholars and immigrants challenged it. In 1916 one journalist noted that as immigrants from an ethnic group became established and prosperous, they tended to seek out the cultural traditions of their homelands. As the immigrants became "… more and more objectively American," he wrote, "they also [became] more and more German or Scandinavian or Bohemian or Polish."

Moving Forward

One important paper for New York's Jewish immigrants was the *Forward*. Founded in 1897, the paper was published in Yiddish. Its circulation reached 175,000, making it the largest foreign-language daily paper in the country. The *Forward* published letters with questions about life in America, and the editors responded with advice. (They did not mention that they created some of the questions as well.)

Although the letters may have helped immigrants *assimilate* (adopt American ways), the overall tone of the *Forward* was not necessarily open to all American values. The paper had a clear political message, as it promoted socialism—a political philosophy that suggested the workers, not wealthy investors, should own and run businesses. Many Jews—and other immigrants—saw socialism as the best way to ensure better economic and political conditions for the working class. Still, even that socialist paper carried an advertisement for Yiddish translations of the U.S. Constitution. The ad said the famous document offered "the high road to citizenship, employment, and success."

The idea that many nationalities and cultures could exist side by side without creating a distinct American ethnic group was called *cultural pluralism*. The first person to discuss the concept was a Jewish-American philosopher named Horace Kallen. To Kallen, cultural pluralism was not only a fact, but also a positive development for the country. He believed America would be stronger as "a democracy of nationalities" where English was the common language but where each group had "its own peculiar dialect or speech, its own individual and inevitable … intellectual forms." Kallen compared America to an orchestra made up of many individual musicians who play the same symphony, rather than a bubbling pot that melted away a person's unique identity.

However, Kallen was in the minority. Most Americans accepted the idea of a melting pot and wanted immigrants to lose their old traditions. For the immigrants themselves the issue was not always so clear. Within families children assimilated fairly easily, while their parents tended to resist. Some ethnic groups, such as the Greeks, formed competing organizations that took opposite stands on how much they should lose their old culture. But at times assimilation happened without any formal decision by the immigrants, since many factors in their lives promoted the process.

Schools

One of the most important social tools for encouraging assimilation was public schooling. Entering the 20th century, in cities such as Chicago and New York up to 75 percent of the public-school students were foreign born. Immigrant children from different ethnic groups were mixed together and learned American cultural ideas, such as the nature of democracy. They also learned English quickly if they wanted to succeed, since classes were rarely taught in foreign languages.

To Americans who welcomed immigrants and their assimilation, the schools were doing great work. In 1903 one reporter visited a New York elementary school attended by children from about 25 different ethnic groups. His conclusion: "There are many things in which, as a rule, the public consider that the public schools fail, but the one thing that cannot be denied—and it is the greatest—is that these boys and girls of foreign parentage catch readily the simple American ideals of independence and individual work and, with them, social progress."

Although many immigrant parents saw the economic and social values of education, public schooling was not welcomed by all. Roman Catholics tended to think that the schools tried to reduce the influence of the church's teachings in the students' lives. Parents sometimes feared their children would stop speaking their native languages and become cut off from their cultures and families.

Other immigrants were more concerned with their children earning money in the present to help the family's finances, rather than studying to get good jobs in the distant future. The idea of social mobility, of the next generations achieving greater success than their parents and grandparents, was not important to some immigrants—at least, not at first. As they became assimilated, second-generation immigrants learned that the belief in social mobility was part of being American.

Newspapers

As the number of immigrants from a particular ethnic group grew, educated and enterprising businesspeople established newspapers for their communities. At various times more than 1,000 foreign-language daily and weekly papers were published. The papers were printed in ethnic groups' native languages, and they kept immigrants informed on developments at home and in the local community. But the papers also provided useful information about life in America. For immigrants who did not speak English, the papers were an important part of the assimilation process.

In 1914 a New York Italian-language paper described the role it played for immigrants: "All that a foreigner comes to know about his new country, he absorbs from reading the varied happenings of each day.... Today it may be the news concerning the strike of the street cleaners that teaches him about labor organizations and that particular branch of the city administration. Tomorrow, by reading a sensational case he will come to understand the functions and the mode of procedure of our courts."

The Workplace

The industrial workplace of the early 1900s brought together workers from many different ethnic backgrounds. Workers tended to associate with members of the same ethnic group and religion, and rivalries sometimes formed between the different groups. Fights between the groups were not uncommon. Some labor unions, however, tried to organize workers by industry or skill and overcome the ethnic divisions. Gradually, the workers saw themselves as part of a unified, multi-ethnic group, using English as their common language. The unions also informed workers about American politics so they could vote to protect their interests. In such ways the workplace aided assimilation for some immigrants.

In some cases employers also helped with assimilation. They started night schools to give immigrants English lessons and introduce them to American culture. For example, in 1908 some mining companies in the Minnesota iron range started classes for their workers. There were 830 immigrants from more than a dozen countries enrolled by 1914. About ten percent were women. Although many were not able to read their own language, they learned how to speak, read, and write in English. As one observer noted, they also were able to "… catch something of the spirit of American institutions and feel more a part of the community in which they work."

The young boys here were employed as drivers in a West Virginia coal mine in 1908. The custom of employing young boys in such dangerous work was one practice that led to the passage of the Child Labor Amendment.

Citizenship

Americans and immigrants alike saw acquiring citizenship as a good way for the foreign-born to assimilate. Citizenship increased the immigrants' loyalty to the United States and let them participate in the political process. To become citizens, immigrants had to learn American history, study the Constitution, and learn some English; all the new knowledge eased assimilation. In 1906 the U.S. government tried to make *naturalization* (becoming a citizen) more efficient, introducing its first major changes to the process in more than 100 years. Now specially trained federal employees helped immigrants apply for citizenship and determined if they were eligible.

Nevertheless, what was efficient and honest to the government officials could still be confusing to immigrants. Some lawyers and American organizations advised immigrants on how to go through the process. The steps included filing the proper papers, attending a hearing in front of a judge, and answering questions in English about the Constitution and U.S. history.

Immigrants themselves also became involved in promoting naturalization, and once again the foreign-language press played an important role in encouraging assimilation. For example, in 1911 a Polish paper in Chicago called on Polish immigrants to embrace American citizenship. "Our country, Poland, certainly will not condemn any of her sons because they have renounced allegiance to the brutal governments of our oppressors in order to accept citizenship under the Star-Spangled Banner, the symbol of freedom and human rights."

■ Race Thinking and the New Nativism

Some Americans wanted to shut the door on new immigrants. In response to the new southern and eastern European immigrants, nativists demonstrated their prejudice and discrimination in new ways while also renewing old prejudices.

Many Americans had long held racist ideas about blacks, Native Americans, and Asians. Starting in the 1880s, some thinkers took their ideas of race to greater extremes, considering different groups of white Europeans as separate races. "Race thinking," as that was sometimes called, fueled anti-immigrant hatred as the new immigrants arrived by the millions in the late 19th and early 20th centuries.

Race thinking and the new classifications of white ethnic groups were supported by many prominent Americans, including ministers, educators, and politicians. At the heart of the theory was the idea that the descendants of the Angles and Saxons were the world's premier race. The Angles and Saxons were ancient tribes from Germany that had invaded England around the 6th century. The race thinkers said Angles and Saxons helped create democratic government in England and promoted ideas of individual liberty. The race thinkers also believed English Protestantism had given people religious freedom, ending the supposed tyranny of Roman Catholicism. The British colonists who settled America then brought their ideas about political and religious freedom with them. When the United States was formed, its culture had deep Anglo-Saxon and Protestant roots. What made the country great, the race thinkers said, was the Anglo-Saxonism that shaped the early republic.

Believers of Anglo-Saxonism saw a threat from the other "races" entering the country from southern and eastern Europe. The familiar nativism of the past combined with the new *pseudo* (phony) science of race thinking to launch new attacks on immigrants. The race thinkers borrowed ideas from real science and applied them to ethnic groups. The notion that people inherited traits—such as hair or eye color—from their parents had become widely known in the 19th century. The race thinkers suggested such traits as promoting democracy or obeying laws were passed on in the same way, and some races were more likely to have certain traits.

The Anglo-Saxons were supposedly born with the love of democracy, while some European immigrants belonged to "revolutionary or communistic races" that threatened to overrun America.

Defenders of the Anglo-Saxons

Josiah Strong and Madison Grant were two of America's most famous race thinkers and defenders of the country's Anglo-Saxon heritage. Their main works were written 30 years apart, showing the lasting power of their brand of prejudice.

Strong, a Congregational minister, wrote *Our Country* in 1885. In his book he argued that the Anglo-Saxons were the most democratic people and thus the highest race in the world. "This race of unequaled energy, with all the majesty of numbers and the might of wealth behind it … will spread itself over the earth." Strong was not opposed to all immigration, although he saw dangers in it. When he wrote his book, the new immigrants from southern and eastern Europe had not yet arrived in large numbers.

The situation was different in 1916 when Madison Grant wrote *The Passing of the Great Race*. Grant was a wealthy New York bachelor who founded the New York Zoological Society. He feared the influence of Jews and others who were not Anglo-Saxon, Teutonic (German), or Nordic (Scandinavian). "These immigrants," he wrote, "adopt the language of the native American, they wear his clothes, they steal his name, and they are beginning to take his women, but they seldom adopt his religion or understand his ideals." Writers like Grant and Strong eventually helped influence lawmakers to limit immigration to the United States.

In the 1890s race thinkers were some of the first Americans to notice the new immigrants reaching the country. The Anglo-Saxonists saw a difference between the new arrivals and the earlier immigrants from northern Europe. The racial differences between the two sets of immigrants, the racists said, explained the problems thought to be related to the new immigrants: poverty, crime, radical political ideas. It was such an atmosphere of prejudice that led wealthy New Englanders to form the Immigration Restriction League to try to reduce the number of "inferior" immigrants with a literacy test. The test would have kept out of the country any immigrants who could not read or write.

To economist Francis A. Walker, president of the Massachusetts Institute of Technology, the race problem came down to numbers: Anglo-Saxon Americans were having fewer children, while the immigrants had large families. Walker feared the immigrants would introduce their cultures and wipe out Anglo-Saxonism by greatly outnumbering native-born Americans. He did not believe the new immigrants could ever adopt Anglo-Saxon values.

Attacks on the Immigrants

The new race thinking, along with existing nativism, led to heated words—and sometimes violence—against many ethnic groups. Anti-Semitism (hostility toward or discrimination against Jews) grew. Italians also fared poorly because of their belief in Roman Catholicism and their large numbers in the surge of poor, uneducated Europeans. On the West Coast it was the Japanese who received the bulk of the anti-immigrant feelings, also fed by race thinking. In some cases Californians believed the Japanese were sent by their government as spies to prepare for a military invasion

of the United States. One writer saw the immigration from southern and eastern Europe helping the Japanese scheme by weakening the country with the arrival of inferior races.

The prejudice against immigrants grew in Congress, where more members began to talk about legally restricting European immigration. In 1907 Congress began its first large study of immigration, led by Vermont Senator William Dillingham. Dillingham's U.S. Immigration Commission issued a report in 1911 that showed the government's acceptance of the idea of old and new immigrants. The report found more desirable qualities in the people who had come from Great Britain and northern Europe than in the new immigrants from eastern and southern Europe. The congressional study, along with the current race thinking, led to discussions on restricting immigration. A Texas representative said, "I would quarantine this Nation against people of any government in Europe incapable of self-government for any reason, as I would against the bubonic plague.... I will admit the old immigration of the English, Irish, German, Scandinavian ... the light-haired, blue-eyed Anglo-Saxons, or Celts ... they were great in their own country and great in our country."

Such comments showed how times had changed in the United States. Some 60 or 70 years earlier, nativists had talked about the negative effects of German and Irish immigrants on America and had wanted to keep them out. But in the following decades those immigrants had assimilated—and now made up a larger number of the country's voters. Politicians could not afford to talk about limiting their immigration or question their

In Defense of the Immigrant

In 1915, after President Woodrow Wilson vetoed a law creating a literacy test for immigrants, the Senate met to debate the veto. With enough votes Congress could pass the bill into law without Wilson's approval . One of the strongest opponents of the test and defenders of the immigrants was Senator James A. Reed of Missouri.

Reed found value in every ethnic group that had recently come under attack in America: Jews, Italians, Greeks, Poles, Czechs. Race thinkers of the day condemned the newcomers as peasants; Reed argued that "the great common people of Europe are infinitely the superior portion of that country." If he were starting a new country in the wilderness, Reed said, he would choose the immigrant to settle it: "There is not an immigrant of the common people who comes to our shores who does not love liberty with a fervor we scarcely possess. He loves and appreciates it because he has been denied it."

Reed and other senators like him carried the day in 1915. The literacy test did not pass—for the time being.

contributions to the country. Nevertheless, on the whole the new immigrants lacked political power and were unwanted by a broad segment of the country.

In 1913 Senator Dillingham submitted the first bill ever to limit immigration from Europe. The number allowed would have been based on the number of people from a particular ethnic group in the United States at the time of the 1910 Census. The bill did not pass, but the battle to restrict immigration was just beginning, and Dillingham's plan would come up again in Congress.

▌ Americanization

As anti-immigrant feelings grew, many Americans put increased attention on assimilating the immigrants already in the country. But in the 1910s the push for assimilation began to change. Many native-born Americans wanted immigrants to immediately drop their old languages and customs and embrace American values. That kind of "forced" assimilation became known as "Americanization" or "100 percent Americanism."

At the time the country had less tolerance for anything foreign, especially as tensions grew in Europe. In 1914 World War I began, pitting England, France, Italy, Serbia, and Russia against Germany, the Austro-Hungarian Empire, and the Ottoman Empire. American public opinion tended to favor England and its allies. Immigrants who came from England's enemies were sometimes treated with suspicion in America. Not surprisingly, immigrants from countries on either side were concerned with the situation at home; some raised money in America for the war effort, while others returned to their homelands to fight. Americans paid increasing attention to the loyalty of the immigrants, especially as fears grew that the United States would enter the war.

The general attitude behind Americanization was that the dominant culture should dictate how and when immigrants cast off their old ways and adopted American values. "Nation building," said Frances Kellor, "is to be in the future a deliberate formative process, not an accidental … arrangement." Kellor, a lawyer and social reformer, was one of the leading forces behind Americanization. Working in New York, she had led the fight there for better education and more social welfare for immigrants. Her push for Americanization stemmed from a genuine concern for immigrants. But she and other Americanizers did not see that their efforts denied the immigrants freedom to assimilate as they wanted— if they choose to at all.

Kellor was head of the National Americanization Committee, whose motto was America First. (That replaced the earlier slogan, Many Peoples, But One Nation.) She was concerned with preparing the country for war as well as Americanizing immigrants, and she recruited businesses to support her efforts. "The Americanization of immigrant workmen," she wrote in 1916, "providing them with American standards of living, and encouraging among them the English language and American citizenship becomes … a national service.…" One industrialist who supported Americanization was carmaker Henry Ford. He started English-language classes that his immigrant workers were required to attend.

Critics of Americanization

Immigrants did not always welcome Americanization. Some saw contradictions between the push for them to become "good" citizens and the treatment they received as immigrants. In 1915 one naturalized immigrant wrote to supporters of Americanization: "Your fathers promised life, liberty, happiness; this is the doctrine of Americanism; you practice … misery.… Your fathers preached the social equality of all men, this is Americanism; you practice class and sectarian prejudice."

A Polish scholar visiting the United States suggested how Americans could truly assimilate his countrymen, rather than forcing them to quickly Americanize: "… [A]bove all, make him actively cooperate in the construction of American life.… Make way for his initiative and develop his spirit of creation.… He will become a real citizen only if you treat him as such."

Most native-born Americans, however, still supported Americanization. The U.S. entry into World War I in 1917 added to the drive. The war also brought many changes for some immigrants and their descendants who thought they were already loyal citizens.

CHAPTER 9
Closing the Door

■ World War I

World War I (1914–1918) was supposed to be "the war to end all wars." For almost three years the United States remained officially neutral, thinking the war was strictly a European conflict. But in 1917, after German submarines attacked U.S. merchant ships, President Woodrow Wilson asked Congress to declare war on Germany and its allies. America, Wilson said, would fight "for the ultimate peace of the world and for the liberation of its peoples ... for the rights of nations great and small and the privilege of men everywhere to choose their way of life and of obedience. The world must be made safe for democracy."

Millions of Americans were soon drafted into the military, including many *naturalized* immigrants (those with American citizenship) and American-born citizens of foreign descent. By then the flow of new immigrants into America had slowed considerably because of the war. From July 1, 1915, to June 30, 1916, a total of about 300,000 immigrants entered the country, compared to 900,000 in the year before the war began. For the decade from 1911 to 1920 immigration fell almost one-third from its peak of about 9 million during the previous ten years.

■ Wartime Suspicions

As the Civil War (1861–1865) had, World War I gave America's immigrants the chance to show their loyalty. But for immigrants from the countries now at war with the United States, the war years were not easy. About 4.6 million immigrants had been born in enemy countries. In 1917 they made up one-third of America's foreign-born population, and many had not become naturalized. The Germans received most of the attention from suspicious Americans. The American press had been whipping up anti-German feelings since the war's start in 1914. The Germans were called "Huns" (the name of an Asian tribe that attacked Europe in the 5th century) and accused of committing horrible acts of violence against European civilians. Even before 1917, the anti-German feelings had sometimes carried over to German Americans. When the United States declared war, life became even more difficult for German Americans—citizens and noncitizens alike.

As soon as Congress declared war, President Wilson used his authority under an existing law to arrest enemy aliens—in that particular case, non-naturalized immigrants from Germany and its allies. The law let the government lock up thousands of enemy aliens—mostly German Americans—at Ellis Island, which served as a jail during the war. Congress also passed new laws to restrict what people said or did during the war. One let the government censor (review the content of) foreign-language newspapers.

Congress took advantage of the war hysteria to finally pass a literacy test for immigrants. Wilson once again vetoed the bill, but now Congress had enough votes to override Wilson's wishes and make the bill law. Under the law all adult immigrants had to be able to read in any language (although an illiterate wife could enter with a literate husband). The 1917 law also forbid all Asian immigrants except those from Japan and the Philippines. The literacy test, however, did not seem to have the large impact its supporters thought it would. For example, from July 1920 to June 1921, only 1,450 immigrants were refused entry because they could not read. But the law showed that Americans were more willing to restrict immigration—something that became even more apparent after the war.

"Liberty Cabbage"

World War I (1914–1918) let loose anti-German feelings never seen before or since in the United States. When the country entered the war in 1917, more than 2.3 million German-born people lived in the United States, and millions more had German roots. Simply by speaking German or having a German name, those immigrants and their descendants were considered possible traitors to the United States.

The hysteria against all things German led Americans to rename sauerkraut "liberty cabbage." In Pittsburgh music by the German composer Beethoven was banned. Some towns banned or even burned books with any German influence. The anti-German feelings also led to violence: one German-American miner in Illinois was wrapped in an American flag and then lynched.

Other Actions

State and local governments and the native-born American public joined the assault on the liberties of Germans. (See "Liberty Cabbage" sidebar.) Even if German Americans were not directly attacked, they faced pressure to show their loyalty to avoid the risk of any danger. Years after the war one German American remembered, "There was an awful lot of hard feelings, you know, [by] those people that weren't German…. We had to buy [war bonds].

We was kind of forced to, because you know if you didn't you then was yellow…."

The wartime fears led some native-born Americans to start their own organizations that tried to find spies or traitors. Most of the alleged traitors were Germans or socialists who opposed the war. One of the patriotic groups, the American Protective League, had government approval to do its work. The league claimed to have 250,000 members, mostly businessmen, who tracked down rumors of disloyalty. In Colorado the league found a German Lutheran minister who at first would not say who he wanted to win the war—Germany or America. He finally said America. The league reported, "he was instructed to prove this by preaching and praying it in private as well as in public, which he agreed to do."

Not all Americans believed the wild anti-German suspicions or accepted the treatment they received. Frederic Howe was commissioner of immigration on Ellis Island during and after the war. He later wrote that many of the Germans under his control "had been arrested by persons with little concern about their innocence or guilt." Howe himself was labeled pro-German. "As I look back over these years," Howe said, "my outstanding memories are not of the immigrants. They are rather of my own people … the state not only abandoned the liberty which it should have protected, it lent itself to the stamping out of individualism and freedom."

After the war some anti-German feelings remained, but they soon faded away. Instead Americans turned their suspicions and hatred on another kind of immigrant: the political radical.

The Red Scare

As the United States was fighting World War I, one of its allies—Russia—was going through tremendous political change. Late in 1917 Russian socialists, led by the Communist Party, or Bolsheviks, took over their country's government. Most European socialists of the day worked within the existing political system to try to change society. The Communists, however, believed in violent revolutions so the world's workers could control the factories and governments. The Russian Revolution created the first communist nation, and it created great fears in the United States, where many immigrants were socialists.

The 1886 Haymarket Square Riot (see Chapter 6) was the most famous instance of socialists and other political radicals stirring American fears. The leaders of the rally that led to the Haymarket riot had been foreigners, and since then many Americans associated socialism and other foreign political movements with immigrants. Immigrants had been active in the labor movement—some business owners and politicians saw them as a threat to America's capitalist tradition, which encouraged investors to take risks with their money and advocated few legal restrictions on how they operated the companies they formed. But not all labor groups were socialist, and few immigrant socialists promoted violent revolution in America. They simply wanted to use the democratic system to improve social and economic conditions for the country's workers.

In the time right after World War I many Americans could not make a distinction between labor groups and real radicals, or between immigrants who were a possible risk to America and the vast majority who were not. The events in Russia convinced some Americans that communists would try to do the same thing in the United States. The Americanization movement and the patriotism of the war years carried over to create another atmosphere of suspicion. Instead of trying to limit the freedom of Germans, the country began to look for Bolsheviks or any other foreign immigrants who seemed to threaten the country's security. Since the symbolic color of Russia's Communist Party was red, the foreign radicals were called Reds, and the crackdown against American radicals between 1919 and 1920 is known today as the Red Scare.

A. Mitchell Palmer, below, was a leader in American efforts to locate suspected radicals during the Red Scare in 1919 and 1920.

Riots and "Palmer Raids"

After the war the United States had approximately 100,000 admitted socialists. Most were immigrants and about two-thirds of them now called themselves communists. The rest still called themselves socialists. In 1919 various socialist and communist groups had their first large, public, postwar gatherings on "May Day" (May 1), an international socialist holiday. They held parades in many major cities, and in most places they were greeted by angry anti-radical protesters. In Boston a riot led to the death of one socialist and the arrest of more than 100 marchers—but none of the attackers were arrested. According to a socialist newspaper in Cleveland, a parade in that city started peacefully but soon turned violent: "Riots and mobs ruled in the downtown section of the city for two hours. Shots were fired, police clubs cracked scores of heads...."

During Prohibition the FBI raided many factories that produced illegal alcohol. Here, agents seize 7,000 barrels of beer in a Newark, New Jersey, raid.

The climate of fear and violence grew after some bombings were carried out against government targets. In June a bomb went off in front of the home of U.S. Attorney General A. Mitchell Palmer, the man who was leading the legal fight against radicals. The bombings were carried out by violent individuals, not one group, but most Americans assumed the bombings were part of a giant plot, backed by Russia, to destroy America.

Palmer asked Congress to give him special powers to find potentially violent radicals. The lawmakers did not go along with Palmer, so he went out on his own, raiding offices and homes where labor and socialist groups met. He managed to deport hundreds of people to Russia after accusing them of being dangerous radicals—sometimes with no proof. In some cases the people Palmer arrested were U.S. citizens. Others were not communists. But for a few months he was able to justify denying the legal rights of Americans in his struggle to end the Red Scare. In February 1920 Palmer wrote, "I have been asked ... to what extent deportation will check radicalism in this country. Why not ask what will become of the United States Government if these alien radicals ... carry out the principles of the Communist Party?"

But as quickly as Palmer caught the public's attention with his raids, the strong anti-radical feelings began to die down. In 1919 several industries had been hit with labor strikes; by 1920 the strikes had ended. Since they had peaceful relations with their workers again, corporate managers no longer felt threatened by socialists. As in the past, they counted on the labor of foreign workers for their industries, so business leaders helped cool the Red Scare. Americans who defended civil liberties (political and social rights), such as journalists and lawyers, also attacked Palmer and his methods. The Red Scare faded away, although general anti-immigrant feelings had not disappeared.

Another Round of Nativism

Even if foreign radicals were no longer a menace, *nativist* (anti-immigrant) Americans still saw problems with the new immigrants. The war had slowed immigration and turned the country's attention to other issues. But by September 1920 about 5,000 immigrants a day were arriving at Ellis Island and familiar patterns of anti-immigrant feelings began to rise. Postwar nativism was largely anti-Semitic (prejudiced against Jews), anti-Catholic, and anti-Italian. Automaker Henry Ford was a leading anti-Semite, publishing attacks on Jews in his company newspaper. (Years later he took back all his statements and publicly apologized for them.)

The anti-immigrant feeling went beyond words. One violent incident took place in 1920 in West Frankfort, Illinois: after a number of robberies and two kidnappings in the town, local citizens put the blame on immigrants. A mob went on a rampage through primarily Italian immigrant neighborhoods. They burned homes, beat the Italians, and drove them from the town.

A new social development in the United States created another barrier between immigrants and the dominant Anglo culture: Prohibition. In 1919 the country adopted a constitutional amendment that outlawed alcohol. Many immigrants came from cultures that accepted alcohol—especially beer and wine—as a normal part of everyday life. American anti-alcohol crusaders, however, had convinced the country that all alcohol was evil. Many immigrants opposed Prohibition, and criminals who tried to evade the anti-alcohol laws were often immigrants. To nativists, the immigrants' beliefs about Prohibition were another sign of their disloyalty to American laws and values.

The return of nativism was also tied to a new interest in race thinking. The ideas of Madison Grant, who wrote about race in the 1910s, gained new popularity. Other writers added their own ideas about the superiority of the Anglo-Saxon (sometimes also called Nordic) race. In the middle of such an atmosphere an old organization gained a new strength: the Ku Klux Klan. When the Klan had first appeared after the Civil War, it targeted Southern blacks and the Northern whites who supported them. The new Klan turned its attention to Jews, Catholics, and immigrants in general, in addition to blacks.

The Klan Reborn

The new version of the Ku Klux Klan spread beyond the South; by 1921 it claimed members in 45 states. Many Americans disliked the Klan and its

In 1964 more than 3,000 Mississippians belonged to the United Klans of America. The Ku Klux Klan often participated in open-air torch burning as well as cross burning.

ideals. William Allen White, a Kansas journalist, saw the Klan recruiting in his town and reported that the citizens had no time for a group he said was based on "… such deep foolishness that it is bound to be a menace to good government in any community." But at its height in 1923 the Klan had up to 3 million members—people who believed they had a duty to drive out anyone who they thought threatened the country.

Anti-Immigrant Crusader

When Albert Johnson entered national politics, he was a small-town newspaper editor in Gray's Harbor, Washington. Johnson first won local fame when he helped lead a citizen army against striking union workers from the area's lumber industry. To Johnson, radical union members and foreigners—sometimes the same people—were ruining America, and he vowed to stop them.

When Johnson ran for the U.S. House of Representatives in 1912, he campaigned as a strong foe of immigrants. After his election he immediately called for excluding all Asian immigrants and limiting European immigration to relatives of people already in America. Even other politicians who wanted immigrant restriction thought Johnson was extreme. In 1919 Johnson became chairman of the House Committee on Immigration and sought a two-year suspension of all immigration. When he could not win support for that position, Johnson backed the 1921 Quota Act and cosponsored the law that made the quota permanent.

In 1927 Johnson showed the *nativist* (anti-immigrant) thinking that had led him and so many others to support immigration restriction. Too many immigrants, he said, had "sprung from races that, throughout the centuries, have known no liberty at all.… Our capacity to maintain our cherished institutions stands diluted by a stream of alien blood.… The day of unalloyed welcome to all peoples, the day of indiscriminate acceptance for all races, has definitely ended."

According to one Klan leader, the "Nordic" influence in white America had created the best race of people in history. But World War I had shown that "millions whom we had allowed to share our heritage and prosperity, and who we had assumed had become part of us, were in fact not wholly so." The disloyal foreign element was threatening America and the Klan had "awakened to the fact that we must fight for our own. We are going to fight—and win!"

The Klan acted as an independent police force out to protect "Nordic" values. Its victims were run out of town, tarred and feathered, or otherwise physically harmed. But after 1923 the Klan lost much of its strength as politicians and other groups began to fight back. Local governments cracked down on their activities, and protesters—Catholics, Jews, and defenders of civil liberties—began attacking their parades and meetings. The U.S. economy was also gaining strength. As in the past, when times were good, people were less hostile toward immigrants.

Still, a weakened Klan did not end the problems for America's immigrants. Congress was about to make the most radical change ever to the country's immigration laws.

■ New Limits

The idea of putting limits on European immigration had first come up before World War I. After the war Congress again addressed the issue, and now there was strong support for restrictions. The Quota Act of 1921 was supposed to last only one year, but Congress soon extended the law until 1924. Under the law the number of immigrants allowed from each European nation was three percent of their population in the United States at the time of the 1910 Census. The total number of Europeans allowed into the country under the quota was about 355,000 per year. The quota did not affect immigration from Canada and Central and South America.

The law was designed to favor old immigrants over new, and it clearly worked. Under the quota about 200,000 immigrants were allowed from Great Britain, Germany, Scandinavia, and the rest of northern and western Europe. The remaining 155,000 came from southern and eastern Europe. Before World War I about 783,000 immigrants from southern and eastern Europe had been entering the country each year, compared to 183,000 from northern and western Europe.

To some people, such as Representative Albert Johnson of Washington, the Quota Act did not go far enough. When Congress debated establishing a new, permanent quota, Johnson led the fight for even tougher restrictions. (See "Anti-Immigrant Crusader" sidebar.) Johnson and his allies won. The Immigration Act of 1924 reduced the number of total European immigrants to about 164,000 per year and favored old immigrants even more than the first quota system had. Each country was allowed to send two percent of its ethnic population in America at the time of the 1890 Census, before the majority of southern and eastern Europeans had arrived. Each country had a minimum quota of 100. The quotas for Europeans did allow for exceptions. Some immigrants, such as religious figures and college professors, could enter without being counted as part of a country's limit. The law ended all Japanese immigration.

The 1924 law also required future changes in the quota based on "national origins"; therefore, Congress had to examine the ethnic backgrounds of all Americans counted in the 1920 Census. Once again, the system favored immigrants from such countries as Great Britain, Ireland, and Germany.

Contributions of New Immigrants

Would America have been much different if a quota system had been in place earlier? Would important foreigners have been turned away, never given a chance to make contributions to the country? No one can say for sure, here is a sampling of some immigrants who might have been shut out if the quota system had been in effect after 1890.

Irving Berlin (Israel Baline)—Russian Jew, arrived in 1892; wrote such popular songs as "God Bless America" and "White Christmas"

Frank Capra—Italian, arrived in 1903; directed many successful movies, including the Christmas classic, *It's a Wonderful Life*

Felix Frankfurter—Austrian Jew, arrived in 1894; became a U.S. Supreme Court justice

Kahlil Gibran—Lebanese, arrived in 1895; wrote the best-selling book, *The Prophet*

Conrad Hubert (Akiba Horowitz)—Russian Jew, arrived in 1890; invented the flashlight

Varazted Kazanjian—Armenian, arrived in 1895; world famous plastic surgeon who operated on badly injured American soldiers after World War I

David Sarnoff—Russian Jew, arrived 1900; founded the RCA electronics company and the National Broadcasting Company (NBC), known as the "father of American television"

Selman Waksman—Russian Jew, arrived in 1910; discovered a treatment for tuberculosis to win the Nobel prize for medicine

Support for the quota laws was strong, although there were some that spoke out against them One Jewish-American leader, Louis Marshall, wrote to President Calvin Coolidge, asking

Sacco and Vanzetti

One of the most famous legal cases in U.S. history involved two Italian immigrants caught up in the anti-radical and anti-Italian feelings of the 1920s. Nicola Sacco worked in a shoe factory; Bartolomeo Vanzetti sold fish. The two men were friends and admitted anarchists. They were arrested for the murder of two men killed during a 1920 robbery in Massachusetts. Sacco and Vanzetti insisted they were innocent, but the mood of the day made it difficult for them to get a fair trial. The state's attorney insulted the Italian defense witnesses and the judge was prejudiced against them.

After they were convicted, the two Italians appealed the verdict for years, and the case became a national issue. During that time someone else confessed to the two murders, but Sacco and Vanzetti remained behind bars. When it was clear he and Sacco were not going to be released, Vanzetti made a long statement in court. He said in part, "I would not wish to a dog or a snake, to the most low and unfortunate creature of the earth—I would not wish to any of them what I have had to suffer for the things I am not guilty of.... I have suffered because I was an Italian, and indeed I am an Italian." Sacco and Vanzetti were executed on August 22, 1927.

him not to sign the Immigration Act of 1924. He said the southern and eastern Europeans being singled out by the bill "… have been industrious and law-abiding and have made valuable contributions to our industrial, commercial and social development … they adopt American standards of living and … are permeated with the spirit of our institutions."

Many immigrants old and new had found the opportunities they had been looking for when they first reached the United States. For new immigrants in particular, the process of *assimilation* (adoption of American ways) was continuing through the second generation. But the 1924 quotas were a reminder of how hard it could be to find acceptance in America.

CHAPTER 10
Troubles Outside and In

■ Tough Times

The quota system did its job; between 1925 and 1930 immigration from Europe was under one million people, compared to slightly more than 1.5 million in the previous four years. The coming years saw even fewer immigrants, but it was not the quota that led to the declining numbers.

Starting in October 1929, the United States entered the Great Depression—its worst economic crisis ever. The stock market crashed, meaning stocks lost their value. Shares in some companies became almost worthless. Wealthy and middle-class Americans lost a lot of money—sometimes all they had. Many more lost their jobs. By the 1930s about 33 percent of the country was out of work. Given the poverty that gripped the nation, few people came to America. In some years more people left than entered as immigrants. Those who left returned to their native lands or sought new homes.

Nevertheless, immigrants were still an issue in the United States during the 1930s. And in the 1940s and 1950s concerns for the legal rights of the country's ethnic and racial minorities—particularly African Americans—paved the way for new thinking about how the dominant culture treated people who did not share its heritage. The dominant whites were sometimes called WASPs—for white, Anglo-Saxon (relating to the ancient German tribes that had settled in England) Protestants. In those decades many immigrants and their descendants still faced prejudice and discrimination as they tried to adjust to American life.

■ Immigration after the Quota

The quota system did not affect Canadian and Mexican immigrants, and they poured into America during the last half of the 1920s. Filipinos and Puerto Ricans were also not included under the quota, since their lands were controlled by the United States. (The United States had won control of the Philippines and Puerto Rico after its victory in the Spanish-American War in 1898. In 1917 Puerto Ricans received American citizenship, so legally they were not immigrants.) Canadians, as in the past, had an easy time *assimilating* (adopting American ways), but the other groups found life more difficult.

Once immigrants were processed at Ellis Island, they bought tickets to various destinations throughout the United States, as shown in this early 1900s photograph of the Ellis Island railroad ticket office.

The Mexicans

Mexican immigration to America started to rise after 1910—the year of the Mexican Revolution. Mexicans ended the rule of a dictator in their country, but the next few years featured civil wars and social disorder. A huge population boom in Mexico and the need for farm workers in the United States (especially during World War I [1914–1918]) drove many Mexicans north. Between 1911 and 1930 almost 700,000 Mexicans legally entered the United States; thousands more did not bother with the paperwork needed to enter and simply walked across the border.

A Mexican father and his children wait for him to be chosen as a day laborer for work on a sugar beet farm in Colorado.

The Mexicans settled mostly in the West and Southwest. They soon became the largest immigrant group in California. Most had to accept low-paying jobs and were treated with hostility, as poor Mexicans in America had been treated since the Mexican-American War (1846–1848). One California educator called them "a menace to the health and morals of the rest of the community." For the most part Mexicans faced equal prejudice in Texas.

The need for Mexican labor fell during the Great Depression and Americans turned even more hostile toward Mexican immigrants. In the 1930s immigrants—and even some Mexican-American citizens—were rounded up and placed in trucks and on trains that took them back to Mexico. An estimated 500,000 people were returned in that way and about half were born in the United States. One Mexican American described the ordeal: "They pushed most of my family into one van.... We drove all day. The driver wouldn't stop for bathroom nor food nor water.... We had always known we were hated. Now we had proof."

In the 1940s, when America was at war with Japan and Germany, U.S. government policy once again welcomed Mexican immigrants. A special program with the Mexican government, called the *bracero* program, brought Mexican farm workers to the country. Such workers, however, were only allowed in America for limited periods of time. The war also brought other opportunities for Mexican Americans, as many were able to leave rural areas and find better-paying factory jobs making weapons for the military. But on the whole Mexican Americans still faced prejudice and discrimination, and they did not make as much money as European immigrants did.

Filipinos and Puerto Ricans

The first significant Filipino immigration began in the early 1900s. Filipinos had a unique status at that time. They were considered U.S. nationals, since their homeland was controlled by the United States. As nationals, they could freely enter America, but they were not citizens. They also could not become citizens, as the country's laws classified them as nonwhites who were not eligible for citizenship.

After the Gentlemen's Agreement (see Chapter 7) with Japan ended the immigration of unskilled Japanese workers, plantation owners in Hawaii began recruiting Filipinos to work in their sugar cane fields. When the 1924 quota system went into effect, mainland employers also turned to Filipino labor. By 1930 more than 45,000 Filipinos lived on the mainland—an increase of almost 40,000 since 1920.

Like the Japanese immigrants before them, the Filipinos worked mostly in agriculture along the West Coast, particularly in California. Over time more Filipinos moved to cities, but they were usually limited to low-paying jobs as domestic servants or restaurant workers. Also like the Japanese, the Filipinos faced racist attitudes. Most Filipino immigrants were men, and they had difficulty finding wives when some states passed laws forbidding them to marry white women. One judge said the immigrants were "scarcely more then savages" and "because Filipinos work for nothing, decent white boys can't get jobs." Individual immigrants were sometimes attacked, and in 1930 a Filipino social center in Stockton, California, was bombed. Four years later Congress passed a law restricting Filipino immigration to just 50 people per year.

The Puerto Ricans were more fortunate, since they had U.S. citizenship. The U.S. government had no restrictions on their immigration. But Puerto Ricans did not come to America in large numbers between the two world wars. By 1940 under 70,000 Puerto Ricans and their descendants lived in America; most were in New York City. The first large wave of Puerto Rican immigration started after World War II (1939–1945).

The Great Migration

One of the largest movements of people within the United States took place during the first third of the 20th century. At a time when Americans were debating how foreigners affected their society, a group of Americans was making an equally important impact on a large section of the country. From 1915 to 1930 an estimated 1.5 million blacks left the South for the cities of the North, Midwest, and West Coast. Many were poor rural sharecroppers who wanted better jobs; others were part of the black middle class who also believed they could find a better life outside of the South. That mass movement of blacks is known as the "great migration."

Although some blacks had started moving north during the 1890s, the first large movement began during World War I. Northern factories needed

During the 1940s, Casita Maria, a Puerto Rican aid society, provided breakfast for youngsters of newly arrived immigrants.

workers, and the jobs paid better than the work available for blacks in the South. In 1917 an African-American minister wrote to the *Chicago Defender,* a black newspaper, explaining the situation in Alabama: "I wish to say that we are forced to go when one thinks of a grown man's wages as only fifty to seventy five cents per day for all grades of work. He is compelled to go where there is better wages and sociable conditions, believe me…. Only a few days ago more than 1,000 people left here for the North and West."

The Baker's Boy

David Dubinsky became interested in the labor movement when he was a young baker living in Lodz, Poland. At 15 he led a strike against local Jewish bakeries—including one owned by his father. Because of his union activities, the Russian officials who ruled Poland sent him to Siberia. Dubinsky escaped, then set out for America.

In New York Dubinsky started working in the clothing industry and soon joined the International Ladies Garment Workers' Union. After holding a number of important positions, Dubinsky became president of the union in 1932. He approved of strikes but was against communism. In 1935 he led a split within the American Federation of Labor (AFL), which included his union among its members. Along with John Lewis of the United Mine Workers, Dubinsky helped form the Committee (later Congress) of Industrial Organizations (CIO). The CIO wanted to unionize unskilled factory workers—largely first- and second-generation immigrants—while the AFL was only interested in skilled craftsmen.

The CIO won the support of auto and steel workers and held a number of strikes. By 1940 the CIO had more than 2 million members. In Dubinsky's own union the garment workers won better wages and shorter hours without needing to strike. Later in his career Dubinsky helped create a merger of the CIO and the AFL.

The blacks who moved north lived very much as the immigrants did. They stayed in tenement buildings in poor neighborhoods of the major cities, usually living close to other blacks. Although some found factory work, others had to take low-paying jobs (still at higher wages than what they were likely to make in the South). With the rising black population in the North, racial tensions grew as well. The North lacked a formal system of Jim Crow laws, but businesses and communities still segregated blacks. During and after the war, deadly race riots broke out in a number of cities, including Chicago; East St. Louis, Illinois; and Tulsa, Oklahoma.

▉ Immigrants in the 1930s

The Great Depression forced the United States to look at the role of government in the nation's economy. The man who began that process was President Franklin D. Roosevelt. The president came from Dutch and French ancestry, and in many ways he was a classic example of the WASP elite. His parents were wealthy and he attended some of the country's best schools. Afterward he quickly won important government positions. But as president, Roosevelt fought for the interests of the common people, including the immigrants. Under him the Democratic Party became the party that most often represented the ethnic and racial groups that felt forgotten by America's dominant WASP culture.

Roosevelt's answer to the Great Depression was a system of programs called the New Deal. The federal government created jobs for millions of people who were out of work. It also began to regulate the stock market and insure the money Americans deposited in banks. Social Security was introduced, providing money for workers after they retired or if they became disabled. Some of the changes upset many Americans, who wanted the government to be as small as possible, but a majority of voters supported Roosevelt and his New Deal.

New Opportunities

For many immigrants the New Deal marked their first chance to move up in American society. The government's new programs created a need for new workers, and second-generation immigrants—particularly Jews and Italians—found better job opportunities than in the past. The U.S. government also sponsored studies of various ethnic groups and their contributions to the country. Americans began to develop a new sense of the important role immigrants had played in building the United States.

The 1930s also saw growth in the labor movement. The Wagner Act of 1935 gave unions greater rights for representing workers. More workers joined unions and organizations such as the Congress of Industrial Organizations (CIO), which united immigrants of various groups in the struggle for better wages and working conditions.

An Old Problem Recurs

Despite such gains, not all immigrants had an easy time during the New Deal era. Jewish Americans were particularly singled out for attacks. Anti-Semitism (hostility toward or discrimination against Jews) was on the rise at the same time that Adolf Hitler was pursuing strong anti-Jewish policies in Nazi Germany. The most visible American anti-Semite of the day was a Roman Catholic priest, Father Charles Coughlin. On a weekly radio show he frequently repeated one of the old stereotypes voiced about the Jews: they controlled America's finances and wanted to use their money to take over the world.

Most Americans ignored the ideas of the new anti-Semites, but the overall mood in the country was not welcoming to Jews, as many trying to flee Europe found out. The rise of Nazism in Germany and that country's increasing military power scared many Jews. They became refugees. Unlike immigrants who leave a country for economic reasons, the Jewish refugees left because they feared they would lose their political and legal rights—or even their lives.

Hundreds of thousands of Jews left Germany and its neighbors; many headed for the United States. Some U.S. officials, however, did little to help Jewish refugees get the visas they needed to enter the country. About 150,000 Jewish refugees did make it to the United States; most were well educated and some, such as Albert Einstein, were world famous. But the average Jew—and even some non-Jewish Germans—had a hard time getting to America.

The economic troubles of the Great Depression and anti-immigrant attitudes made the United States unwilling to relax its laws on immigration. Fears of new arrivals were also tied to political developments in the country. During the 1930s many Americans—native-born and immigrant—took a new interest in socialism. They believed socialism or Russian-style communism would solve the country's economic problems. Although the government did not repeat its tactics from the 1920 Red Scare, Americans were suspicious of foreigners who might have socialist beliefs. In 1940 Congress passed the Smith Act, which gave the government the power to deport *alien* (noncitizen) communists and required alien residents to register with the government each year.

■ World War II

When the Smith Act was passed World War II had already started in Europe and Asia in 1939. The United States was able to stay out of the conflict until December 7, 1941, when Japan launched a sneak attack on the U.S. Naval base at Pearl Harbor, Hawaii. The next day President Franklin Roosevelt asked Congress to declare war on Japan and three days later America declared war on Japan's allies—Italy and Germany—as well. Unlike what had happened during World War I, German immigrants and their descendants were not called "un-American." The Italians also escaped any prejudice, and members of both ethnic groups served in the military. The situation was quite different for Japanese Americans, however.

Americans of Japanese descent arrive at the Seattle assembly center where they were detained as possible enemies of the state during the 1940s.

Bitter Years for the Japanese

After Japan bombed Pearl Harbor many white Americans believed Japanese Americans would support their former

homeland during the war. They feared the Japanese would sabotage U.S. war efforts. The attack also brought back the old racist attitudes against the Japanese that were common on the West Coast. One general said, "the Japanese race is an enemy race and while many second and third generation Japanese born on United States soil, possessed of United States citizenship, have become 'Americanized,' the racial strains are undiluted."

In February 1942 President Franklin Roosevelt gave in to that kind of race thinking. He signed an order that placed more than 110,000 Japanese Americans—most of them U.S. citizens—in relocation centers. (The order did not effect Japanese Americans living in Hawaii.) Describing life at a California center, one Japanese American wrote, "You felt like a prisoner.... You're kept inside a barbed-wire fence, and you know you can't get out."

Opponents of the centers compared them to the concentration camps the Nazis used to imprison Jews and other ethnic groups. Many Japanese Americans had to sell their businesses, land, and most of their possessions before they moved to the centers. With few exceptions the Japanese quietly accepted their fate and marched off to the centers. But although their families were forced to give up their belongings and were locked in the camps, many second-generation Japanese wanted to prove their loyalty. They asked to fight for the United States in the war. In 1943 President Roosevelt approved the creation of an all-Japanese combat unit—the 442nd Regiment. The 442nd saw its first action in Europe in 1944 and fought bravely in many battles, suffering high rates of injury and death.

By the war's end in 1945 the men of the 442nd had won more military decorations for bravery than any other U.S. fighting unit.

In December 1944 the Supreme Court ruled that the government had no right to prevent loyal U.S. citizens of Japanese or any other descent from moving about as they wished. The relocation centers were closed soon after. But Japanese Americans had already faced extreme discrimination and hardship and they would fight for many years to make the government apologize. In 1988 Congress finally passed a law officially apologizing for the wartime camps and paid $20,000 to each of the approximately 60,000 survivors.

Racial Problems

World War II brought more African Americans into northern cities looking for jobs. They also served in the military: about one million blacks fought for the United States, although they were forced to serve in segregated units. Many blacks saw a contradiction in their wartime experience. The U.S. government said African Americans were fighting to smash foreign dictatorships and preserve democracy, yet the blacks were denied full legal rights in their own country. In Tennessee African Americans asked for blacks to be included on local draft boards. The state's governor replied, "This is a white man's country.... The Negro had nothing to do with the settling of America."

In 1941 black leaders planned a march on Washington, D.C., to protest discrimination in the workplace. They called off the march when President Roosevelt issued an order banning racial discrimination in the country's defense plants. But America could not avoid racial conflict at home while it was waging war overseas.

At some military bases white and black soldiers clashed. In the South white civilians sometimes attacked black military men. Race riots broke out in cities across the United States just as they had during World War I. In 1943 there were riots in 47 cities. The worst was in Detroit, where 35 people died—25 of them black. That year in California Mexicans were also the victims of racial attacks.

Racial Progress

Racial minorities did see some gains during the war years. For the first time ever blacks were allowed to train as airplane pilots. A group trained at the Tuskegee Institute in Alabama was known as the "Tuskegee Airmen." Serving in all-black squadrons, the airmen fought bravely in Europe. Right before the war the U.S. Army appointed its first black brigadier general, Benjamin O. Davis. On the homefront the nation's premier civil rights organization, the National Association for the Advancement of Colored People (NAACP), gained 400,000 new members during the war. A second important group, the Congress for Racial Equality (CORE), was formed in 1942. More blacks—and some whites—saw a growing need to confront racism in America.

Chinese Americans also saw some improvement in their positions. China was an ally of the United States against Japan, and some Americans argued that it was time to repeal the Chinese Exclusion Act of 1882. Congress restored Chinese immigration—

although the quota was set at only 105—and for the first time ever Chinese immigrants were allowed to become American citizens.

Wartime Wrong Finally Made Right

The Medal of Honor is America's highest award for wartime bravery. None of the blacks who fought during World War II (1939–1945) ever received one. Apparently, some white field commanders altered reports about the brave acts performed by blacks; some recommendations for medals landed in the garbage. For years after the war black veterans called for an investigation to determine if racism had kept them from winning any of the 433 Medals of Honor awarded.

In 1993 a federal committee said that a general pattern of racism in the military had denied some African Americans from being honored. Seven veterans were eventually named as deserving the medal, but only one—Vernon Baker—was still alive. On January 13, 1997, at a White House ceremony, Baker and family members of the other six black soldiers received the medals from President Bill Clinton. After receiving his, a tearful Baker said, "The only thing I can say to those who were not here with me today is: thank you, fellows. Well done. I will always remember you."

The war also seemed to create a greater sense of cooperation between America's different white ethnic groups. War movies of the era—and later times—often showed units with members from almost every European ethnic group fighting side by side. Such ethnic mixes are now sometimes seen as comical because they seem so exaggerated, but they were true to life. In 1942 a Polish-American soldier wrote about his unit: "The chief binding force, naturally, is common membership in the army.... An 'Englishman,' a 'Welshman,' a 'Slovak,' and a 'German' make up one of the most joked-about cliques in the company and are always playing cards together. My best friends are a 'Canadian Englishman,' an 'Englishman,' a 'Pole,' a 'Welshman,' a 'Slovak,' a 'Jew,' and a 'German.'"

Postwar Developments

Many U.S. military personnel returning from Europe and Asia after World War II had found wives and husbands while they were overseas. Their desire to bring their spouses—and sometimes children—to America led to a new immigration law. The War Brides Act of 1946 let about 120,000 immigrants enter the country outside of the quota system. Those people included many Japanese women who were still technically excluded from coming to America under the old 1924 immigration law. The larger immigrant issue, however, concerned refugees from the devastated countries of Europe.

Displaced Persons

The war had forced millions of Europeans to leave their homes and go to other countries. Some—like the victims of Nazi Germany—had been forced into concentration camps hundreds of miles from their homes. Others had left on their own to avoid the fighting or the threat of being placed in the German camps. When the war ended, many of those refugees, often called "displaced persons" (DPs), had no homes to which they could return because of the war's destruction. Others did not want to go home for political reasons. The Soviet Union (the name for Russia and its lands from 1922 to 1991) had taken control of large parts of Eastern Europe and set up communist governments under its control. People opposed to communism became displaced persons rather than live under that political system.

Of all the countries that fought during the war, the United States emerged as the richest and strongest. Many Americans felt the nation had an obligation to help some of the war refugees. Other Americans were still not willing to open the door to everyone who wanted to come. In December 1945 President Harry S. Truman let 40,000 refugees into the country on an emergency basis, but it took almost three more years for Congress to set up an official policy on displaced persons.

The Displaced Persons Act of 1948, and a later version passed in 1950, allowed about 410,000 refugees into America over a four-year period. The original law favored people from Germany and discriminated against eastern European Jews. Truman, although he signed the bill, called it "callous" for its treatment "against displaced persons of the Jewish faith." Even the Holocaust, Nazi Germany's slaughter of 6 million innocent Jews, did not end American anti-Semitism. The 1950 version of the law was more favorable to Jews, but an average of just 20,000 a year were allowed into the United States between 1946 and 1952.

The McCarran-Walter Immigration Act

While Congress was addressing the refugee problem, it was also taking its first comprehensive look at immigration since the Dillingham Commission of 1907. In 1950 a Senate committee suggested taking all the existing laws on immigration and *naturalization* (citizenship) and combining them into one new law. The result of that recommendation was the 1952 McCarran-Walter Act, named for its sponsors: Senator Patrick McCarran of Nevada and Representative Francis Walter of Pennsylvania.

The McCarran-Walter Act kept the old national origins plan and quota system in place. Thinking the bill was too restrictive, President Truman vetoed it. "The greatest vice of the present quota system," he wrote, "... is that it discriminates, deliberately and intentionally, against many of the peoples of the world.... The basis of this quota system was false and unworthy in 1924. It is even worse now."

Congress passed the bill over Truman's veto. Although the quota system was still in place, the new law did make some changes to it. The system now favored skilled immigrants and the relatives of U.S. citizens. The McCarran-Walter Act also had some important, positive effects for immigrants. For the first time non-Chinese Asians were allowed to become naturalized citizens and were included in the quota. The law also provided greater gender equality—now female citizens could bring in alien husbands outside of the quota.

Under the 1952 quota about 150,000 immigrants were allowed each year. The actual number who entered, however, was much greater, because more non-quota immigrants came than officials expected. Events in communist nations also led to help for refugees. After the failure of a 1956 rebellion against Hungary's communist government, the United States accepted about 40,000 Hungarian refugees. In the following decade hundreds of thousands of Cubans came to the United States outside of the quota system. The refugees fled a communist takeover in their homeland. Generally, people from nations under communist rule or who were anti-communist themselves were welcomed, because at the time the United States was in a struggle with the communist Soviet Union. America and the Soviet Union were competing to spread their political and military influence around the world—a conflict known as the Cold War.

Growing Comfort for Some

For second- and third-generation immigrants the 1950s brought better times. Thanks to a law known as the G.I. Bill, returning soldiers received money to go to college. For the first

The Hungarian girl shown here, like many of her countrymen, fled her country to avoid Russian repression in 1956. Here, she waits at a refugee camp in Austria, hoping to come to the United States.

time many immigrant families saw sons and daughters earn college degrees and find professional jobs. The economy across the country was booming, and suburbs were growing outside of cities. During the decade between 1 and 2 million new homes were built every year. In the suburbs, immigrants who might have come from neighborhoods dominated by one ethnic group now lived close to members of other immigrant groups. Old ethnic differences and rivalries declined in the atmosphere of increasing wealth and better education. Marriages between

people of different ethnic and religious backgrounds increased, which also eased old tensions.

The decrease in immigration since the 1920s played a part in the era of increased assimilation. Foreign-born people were a much smaller portion of the American population: just under seven percent, compared to almost 15 percent in 1910. WASPs did not feel as threatened by immigration. And with fewer new arrivals from any single ethnic group, members of the groups already in the United States lost some of their old cultural ties, which eased assimilation. The patriotism created during World War II also gave immigrants a stronger sense of being American.

The Cold War also played a part in ending ethnic tensions and boosting assimilation. Many immigrants and their descendants came from countries now under Soviet control: Hungary, Poland, Lithuania, Ukraine, Czechoslovakia. People from such countries were strong opponents of communism and the Soviets, so their patriotism was usually not questioned. Only people who held communist beliefs ran the risk of being called "un-American."

However, the increased assimilation did not mean immigrants cut off all their ethnic ties. In a way, the sense of being accepted by the dominant culture made it easier for third-generation immigrants to keep some parts of their ethnic identities alive without fear of being called disloyal. They could show pride in their roots—the foods, languages, and celebrations of their grandparents' native lands. Cultural pride grew even stronger in the following decades.

Racial Conflict and the Civil Rights Movement

Unfortunately, assimilation was still a problem for African Americans. In the South, Jim Crow laws still created two distinct societies—one black and one white. The situation was only somewhat better in the North. The federal government, under President Truman, took the first steps toward integration during the Korean War (1950–1953). For the first time ever in the U.S. Armed Forces, white and black soldiers fought side by side. But outside of the military, blacks were still denied full legal rights and an equal chance to pursue the "American Dream" as white immigrants did.

In the 1950s groups like the NAACP and CORE led the way in the creation of the civil rights movement. The movement used the courts and public protest by both blacks and whites to demand changes in American society. The most important legal decision came in 1954, in the case of *Brown v. Board of Education*. (See "Segregation: The Beginning of the End" sidebar.) But the struggle for civil rights was fought by individuals as well—African-American men and women who refused to be treated as inferior any longer.

In 1955 a woman named Rosa Parks sat in the back of a Montgomery, Alabama, bus. Across the South blacks were forced to sit at the rear of buses and had their own cars on trains. When a white man asked for Parks's seat because the white section of the bus was full, she refused to give it up. Parks wrote later, "… he spoke again and said, 'You'd better make it light on yourself and let me have those seats….' A few minutes later two policemen got on the bus…. I told them I didn't think I should have to stand up. After I had paid my fare and occupied my seat, I didn't think I should have to give it up. They placed me under arrest then."

Segregation: The Beginning of the End

Starting in the 1930s, black Americans began a new legal assault on Jim Crow laws and segregation. The National Association for the Advancement of Colored People (NAACP) led the way, challenging laws in both state and federal courts. Some small victories paved the way for a major setback to Jim Crow.

In 1948 the federal government supported the NAACP in a case regarding the restriction of the sale or use of property based on race. Two years later the Supreme Court overturned a law segregating students in law schools. Finally, in 1954 the court brought desegregation down to the public schools as well during the case of *Brown v. Board of Education*.

The ruling in *Brown* actually combined legal cases from four different states: Kansas, South Carolina, Virginia, and Delaware. In each case black students were suing for the right to attend integrated public schools. Chief Justice Earl Warren, writing for a unanimous court, said, "In the field of public education, the doctrine of 'separate but equal' has no place. Separate educational facilities are inherently unequal." Those separate facilities could also create in young African Americans "a feeling of inferiority … that may affect their hearts and minds in a way unlikely ever to be undone."

The ruling in *Brown* had an impact beyond schools, as gradually all Jim Crow laws were overturned. But the process to end segregation was not always as fast—or as peaceful—as many Americans, white and black, could have hoped.

After Parks's arrest, the blacks of Montgomery *boycotted*—refused to use—the city's buses. Her actions became a symbol of the peaceful protest that black leaders such as Martin Luther King Jr. believed would help African Americans win their legal rights. In 1963 King was arrested in Birmingham, Alabama, after leading a protest march. While in jail he wrote, "Nonviolent direct action seeks to create such a crisis and establish such creative tension that a community that has constantly refused to negotiate is forced to confront the issue."

Marches, "sit-ins," and rallies were the tools of the civil rights movement. Although the protests were peaceful, sometimes the white authorities in the South were not. Police attacked protesters or stood by as citizens did the job. Civil rights workers were killed and black churches and homes were bombed. The violence appalled most Americans and helped convince Congress that something had to be done. In 1964 and 1965 the government passed a constitutional amendment and various laws designed to protect civil rights and end discrimination against blacks. Blacks could no longer be prevented from voting, and they were assured of equal opportunities to find housing and jobs. The laws gave African Americans the legal power to fight injustice, even if they could not erase all racial prejudice.

The success of the civil rights movement spurred political activity by other groups. Native Americans, women, and Mexicans also used marches and rallies to try to improve their positions in society. Not all the protests were peaceful, and toward the end of the 1960s a small number of African Americans believed they needed to wage an armed revolution to achieve their goals. But most blacks and other protesters did not use violence. The fight for civil rights showed the power of direct but peaceful action to bring changes to the United States.

CHAPTER 11
Immigration on the Rise

The End of the Quotas

At the same time the civil rights movement was beginning to change the status of blacks, immigration to America was changing too. In 1963 President John F. Kennedy had asked Congress to consider changing the national origins and quota system for immigration. After Kennedy's death President Lyndon Johnson continued those efforts, and Congress responded with the Immigration Act of 1965. The bill still set an overall limit of legal immigration: 120,000 for the Western Hemisphere (North and South America) and 170,000 for the Eastern Hemisphere (the remaining continents). No country could send more than 20,000 immigrants per year.

The application process for entry visas still favored people based on their job skills and relations to people already in the United States. But the law ended both the preference for northern and western Europeans and the low limits for people from Asia. In support of the bill President Johnson said, "In establishing preferences, a nation that was built by the immigrants of all lands can ask those who now seek admission, 'What can you do for your country?' But we should not be asking 'In what country were you born?'"

The 1965 act led to an increase in immigration from Asia, Africa, and Latin America. Some arrivals—particularly Asians and Africans—were skilled professionals who wanted better job opportunities, but many unskilled people from poorer nations also took advantage of the new law. Once a few members of a family came, they set off what one historian called "a chain migration of relatives." Immigrants sponsored their relatives, who sponsored more relatives, and the pattern continued, bringing more immigrants to the United States.

Since the law granted exceptions to the 290,000 worldwide quota, legal immigration to the United States reached 323,000 in 1966. More than 100,000 came from Central and South America and another 40,000 came from Asia. Immigrants from such regions outnumbered European immigrants—a trend that has continued ever since.

President Lyndon Johnson signs a new immigration bill in 1965 on Liberty Island in New York City.

Asian Refugees

In the 1960s and into the 1970s the United States was involved in its longest war effort ever during the Vietnam War (1964–1975). The war was a result of the Cold War: the United States supported the South Vietnamese, who wanted a democratic government, and Russia and China backed the communists who ruled in the north. The U.S. government feared that if the North Vietnamese took over South Vietnam, all of Southeast Asia might come under communist rule. The war eventually spread to the neighboring countries of Laos and Cambodia. In 1975 North Vietnam finally won the war—two years after most U.S. troops had left the south. North Vietnam's victory set off the largest wave ever of refugees to America.

From 1952 to 1974 fewer than 19,000 people came from Vietnam, Cambodia, and Laos to the United States. In just the first two months after the war's end, about 131,000 Vietnamese came to America. Many Americans felt a sense of responsibility toward the Vietnamese, since the United States had been allied with them during the war. Others opposed accepting the refugees.

A group of South Vietnamese dependents of U.S. citizens waits at Clark Air Base in the Philippines for permission to immigrate.

Under Presidents Gerald Ford and Jimmy Carter various refugee programs let in about 400,000 Southeast Asian refugees between 1975 and 1979. Some of the people were also from Cambodia and Laos, and not all were direct victims of the Vietnam War. In Cambodia the communist government of Pol Pot terrorized its own citizens, killing at least one million people. A 1978 war between Vietnam and Cambodia ended Pol Pot's reign but created more refugees, as did fighting the next year between Vietnam and China.

"Boat People" and Life in America

Reaching the United States was not easy for many of the Vietnamese, Cambodians, and Laotians. They had to sell all their belongings to pay for the boat trips out of Vietnam to refugee camps in Hong Kong, Thailand, or Malaysia. The boats were often poorly made, and on the waters the refugees were easy victims for pirates. The Vietnamese who made such difficult voyages were sometimes called "boat people." At the camps the refugees had to wait for permission to come to America while living in dirty, crowded conditions.

Once in America, the first Vietnamese arrivals had some advantages. Many came from the middle class and were educated; some spoke English. But in their new home they had to take whatever jobs they could find. Most also had to find sponsors— Americans who would help support them. Church groups across the country sponsored immigrant families, helping them adjust to life in America.

Many Vietnamese, like other Asians before them, opened small shops and restaurants. Their children quickly *assimilated* (adapted American ways), learning English and usually doing well in school. But life was harder for other refugees. Some came alone, since their closest relatives had died in the war.

Later immigrants who came after 1980 had less education. One group of Southeast Asians—the Hmong of Laos—came from a rural life that was very different from what they found in the United States. One U.S. refugee official said their experience was "like going to Mars and starting all over again."

The Latin Americans

Latin America refers in general to the lands where the Spaniards set up colonies in the 16th and 17th centuries: Central and South America and the Caribbean. Other European countries also ruled lands in those regions, but the Spanish influence was the greatest. Latin Americans who speak Spanish are often called Hispanics, although Mexicans are usually called Chicanos. Of all the Latin American countries, Mexico had always sent the most immigrants to America. That did not change after 1965, but when the new immigration law was passed, the Mexicans were joined by more immigrants from the region.

From 1971 to 1980 more than 637,000 Mexicans legally entered the United States. Another 416,000 immigrants came from South and Central America and the Caribbean. The Dominican Republic—a small Caribbean nation—sent a large number of those immigrants: 148,000. The next decade the number of Latin American immigrants exploded as more than 3.7 million entered the United States. More than 1.6 million of those Hispanic immigrants were from Mexico, and today Mexicans make up the largest group of foreign-born Americans.

Despite their rising numbers, Mexicans were slow to take advantage of educational and political opportunities in the United States. Many Mexicans planned to return to Mexico (and many did), so they did not become *naturalized* (become citizens) at the same rate as European immigrants had. Discrimination in American schools and a need to earn money forced many Mexicans to drop out before finishing high school. By 1987 just 45 percent of Mexican Americans over the age of 25 had high school diplomas. Earlier Mexican immigrants had lived mostly in rural areas, but by the 1970s most lived in cities, although many still depended on farm jobs for their work.

Most of the other new Latin American immigrants were poor, and they settled across the country. New York drew most of the South Americans, Dominicans, and other people from the Caribbean, while California and Texas were popular destinations for Mexicans and other Central Americans. Generally, the Latin Americans went wherever they could find jobs. In the cities they often worked as servants, janitors, or other low-paid employees. Some had to work more than one job to survive, but America remained a land of opportunity for such immigrants. "I wanted something better for myself and I found it," one Peruvian immigrant said. "But life will be much better for my sons. They can do anything they want.... I know their lives will be good."

Puerto Ricans

As American citizens, Puerto Ricans were not affected by the Immigration Act of 1965. Their numbers had already been on the rise. About 225,000 lived in the United States in 1950; by 1960 that number had almost tripled, to 615,000. Most settled in New York City and other cities of the Northeast. Many went back and forth between the mainland and their native island. Despite the advantage of being citizens, Puerto Ricans had two distinct obstacles in the United States—a lack of education and racial prejudice.

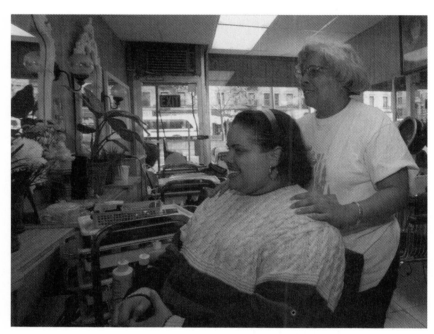

After immigrating from the Dominican Republic, Yolanda Luciano (right) opened her own beauty shop in New York City, shown here in 1997.

Until the 1950s Puerto Rico's economy was based almost totally on agriculture. The island's population was largely rural and uneducated. When they came to America, most Puerto Ricans had to take unskilled jobs, just as millions of immigrants before them had. Although more second- and third-generation Puerto Ricans in the United States began to go to college and get better jobs, poverty rates for the entire group remained high. As in the past, some native-born Americans assumed the poverty was a result of the immigrants' character, not of larger social and economic conditions. The perception created prejudice against Puerto Ricans.

The prejudice was increased by racism. Puerto Ricans vary greatly in skin color—the result of hundreds of years of intermarriage between whites and blacks on the island. Darker Puerto Ricans often faced the same kind of racial discrimination African Americans had always endured in the United States. Lighter-skinned Puerto Ricans had an easier time assimilating into American culture, if they chose to do so.

Cubans

One unique group of Hispanic immigrants was the Cubans. They—like many Southeast Asians—were refugees fleeing a communist revolution in their homeland. Just 90 miles off the coast of Florida, Cuba had a close relationship with the United States before Fidel Castro led a revolution against the ruling government in 1959. The first wave of refugees left shortly afterward.

Most of the refugees were white and middle class, and many expected to return to Cuba as soon as the United States helped end Castro's revolution. That day never came, and more Cubans arrived in America. About 800,000 came between 1960 and 1990. The majority of the Cubans settled in Florida, particularly in and around Miami. By the 1980s they had elected a Cuban-American mayor in that city and were successful in business. In 1989 Ileana Ros-Lehtinen was the first Cuban American elected to Congress—and one of just a handful of first-generation immigrant women ever elected.

Since they became such a large proportion of the population of southern Florida, the first Cuban arrivals could keep much of their culture intact; and because they were white and educated, they could also assimilate fairly easily when they wanted.

A second round of Cuban refugees had a harder time finding jobs and assimilating in America. In 1980 Castro let about 130,000 people leave Cuba for the United States. Most sailed from the port of Mariel, so they were called Marielitos. Unlike the first refugees, those Cubans were mostly black and unskilled. Some had mental disabilities and others were prisoners Castro deliberately sent to America. A few thousand of the Marielitos were not welcomed by the U.S. government and had to stay in detention camps for years; some eventually went back to Cuba. Most of the Marielitos, however, received federal and state assistance and were allowed to stay.

▓ Illegal Immigration

Starting in the 1970s and continuing through the 1980s, illegal immigration was one of America's hottest political issues. Illegal immigrants (also called undocumented aliens) were not new: in the early 19th century slave traders illegally brought Africans into the country after Congress had outlawed the slave trade. After the 1924 quota law was passed some immigrants snuck into the country from Mexico and Canada or forged papers to get visas. In the 1950s the U.S. government carried out a campaign to find and deport Mexicans illegally working in the Southwest.

The modern illegal immigrants were mostly from Latin America, although some were European. (Irish visitors, in particular, often stayed in the country illegally after entering on short-term tourist or student visas.) The border

between Mexico and the United States stretches for 2,000 miles. The Immigration and Naturalization Service (INS) is the federal agency that handles immigration issues and patrols the border, but it lacked (and still lacks) enough officers to guard all of it. In the 1970s the border became a magnet, drawing poor Mexicans and other Central American immigrants who wanted to enter the United States but did not qualify under the new quota system. Others entered the country legally as tourists, then simply moved in with relatives and found jobs.

Confronting Illegal Immigration

By 1980 New York City and Los Angeles were the typical homes for illegal immigrants. In New York they made up an estimated ten percent— about 750,000—of the city's population. Some people—particularly business owners who needed cheap labor—welcomed the illegal immigrants. "Without the Mexicans," one California garment maker said, "our factory would have to shut down. If they don't find a way to get across, we'll help them." Some economists claimed illegal immigrants merely took the kinds of low-paying jobs that most Americans refused to take but were necessary for the country to function.

Many native-born citizens, however, grew alarmed at the number of illegal immigrants. One political columnist wrote in 1986, "So many Mexicans are crossing U.S. borders illegally that Mexicans are reclaiming Texas, California, and other territories that they have long claimed the Gringos [Anglos] stole from them." Americans complained that illegal immigrants took away jobs from poor Americans who were on welfare. The immigrants also used the medical and educational systems, and American taxpayers resented paying for such services for people who were technically criminals.

New immigrant laws allow illegal aliens to qualify for permanent residency. Here, Hector Marroquin, who has been fighting deportation since 1977, hands in his papers for legal status under the new laws.

To address illegal immigration in 1986, Congress passed the Immigration Reform and Control Act (IRCA). The law let illegal immigrants who had entered the country before 1982 become legal *aliens* (noncitizens). That was called the *amnesty* part of the law—the forgiving of a past crime. The immigrants could then apply for citizenship if they desired. But the law made it harder for new illegal immigrants to work in the United States. Employers had to verify that their employees were not illegal immigrants. Companies that knowingly hired undocumented workers would be fined. Under the amnesty program more than 3 million immigrants applied for legal status, and almost 70 percent of them were from Mexico. Salvadorans and Guatemalans were the next most likely to apply for amnesty.

A few years after the amnesty program was introduced, illegal immigration began to rise again. Just four years after passing the IRCA, Congress again addressed immigration reform and illegal aliens. The Immigration Act of 1990 actually expanded legal immigration, setting a limit of 675,000 per year as of 1995. Like earlier laws, the quota favored immigrants with professional skills or family ties to people already in the United States. The law also created a lottery that awarded green cards to illegal immigrants and potential immigrants. The cards allowed noncitizens to live and work permanently in America.

■ The Return of Anti-Immigrant Feelings

Thanks to the Immigration Act of 1965 and a policy of welcoming most refugees, immigration soared. Between 1981 and 1990 more than 7.3 million came to America—the second-highest total ever for one decade. Only the period from 1901 to 1910 had more: almost 8.8 million. The legal immigrants of the 1980s were joined by an estimated 2.75 million illegal immigrants. Just as in the 1910s, more Americans began to question whether the country could absorb so many new people.

Some of the arguments against immigration were economic, as they had been in the past. In 1981 a government commission studied immigration and refugee policies. The commission's leader said, "During the next 15 years ... the United States will create about 30 million new jobs. Can we afford to set aside more than 20 percent of them for foreign workers?

No. It would be a disservice to our own poor and unfortunate." But the attack on immigration also took racist tones. Most of the new immigrants were Asian and Hispanic. The Hispanics especially stirred the concern of native-born Americans, who saw them as poor and unwilling to learn English. The Hispanics were also targeted because they made up the bulk of the illegal immigrants. More Americans began to talk about the need to clamp down on illegal immigration. Some began to discuss restricting all immigration.

A New Nativism?

Some of the reaction to the increased immigration was also a response to the rise of *multiculturalism* in American society. Multiculturalism is primarily an educational and social movement. It encourages every racial and ethnic group to take pride in its historical accomplishments and stresses that American culture is a mixture of the traditions of all those groups. Multiculturalism developed from the older notion of *cultural pluralism* (the idea that many nationalities and cultures could exist side by side without creating a distinct American ethnic group) which attacked the idea of immigrants "melting" into an American culture that was primarily white and Anglo. The immigrants who came after 1965 had added even more racial and ethnic diversity to the mix.

By the 1980s many native-born Americans felt multiculturalism in the schools did not reflect the reality of America's past. For good or bad, the opponents of multiculturalism claimed, America's culture was traditionally Anglo. Supporters of multiculturalism

thought such "traditionalists" ignored the importance of ethnic groups and denied them their place in contemporary American society.

The police separate pro- and anti-Proposition 187 marchers in the Westwood section of Los Angeles in August 1996.

A few scholars labeled the opponents of immigration and multiculturalism "new nativists." Some of the opponents had racist tendencies as past *nativists* (people with anti-immigrant feelings) had. But the United States had a different social climate than in the early part of the century. After the civil rights movement and increased tolerance for different ethnic and racial groups among the general public, few nativists would openly express racist ideas. Nativists and others who questioned increased immigration were more likely to talk about cultural problems posed by immigrants. One U.S. senator said, "A substantial portion of these new persons and their descendants do not assimilate satisfactorily into our society.... Furthermore, if language and cultural separation rise above a certain level, the unity and political stability of our nation will—in time—be seriously eroded."

English Only

Some Americans who opposed multiculturalism belonged to ethnic and racial groups that had faced past discrimination. That was the case with S.I. Hayakawa, a Japanese American who addressed one of the main concerns of the new nativists: language.

In 1981 as a U.S. senator, Hayakawa introduced a constitutional amendment to make English the official language of the nation. Hayakawa was bothered by the introduction of *bilingual* (two-language) and multicultural education and the use of bilingual ballots. Such changes, he felt, reflected a dangerous cultural trend. He thought national unity was shattered when people identified themselves as "Chinese-Americans," "African-Americans," or other ethnic and racial "hyphens." "We're all American, aren't we?" he asked. "What do we do when the 300 nationalities, languages and cultures in our country decide to get identity-hyphenated. How about that for a mess? I hope our English language amendment will reverse the need for ethnic identity."

In 1983 Hayakawa helped start a group called U.S. English to promote English as America's official language. Three years later a second group was formed, called English First. Both groups support a national official-language law and the ending of bilingual education and ballots. Their efforts are sometimes called the "English-only" movement.

Legal groups, the National Education Association, labor unions, and various Hispanic organizations have led the charge against English only. The American Federation of Labor and Congress of Industrial Organizations (AFL-CIO), the nation's leading labor group, said, "Newly arriving immigrants, and even some who have lived in this country for years, might fail to acquire fluency in English but still have a contribution to make to American society.... Americans who think the English language needs the law to bolster its position betray a strange lack of confidence in its influence and appeal. English is already our common language."

The English-only movement, illegal immigration, multiculturalism, and the size of legal immigration remain crucial issues in the 1990s. If anything, the debates over them grow sharper. But unlike in 1924, when Congress easily passed the first quota system, Americans seem less sure about how such issues should be settled.

CHAPTER 12
Into the 21st Century

◾ Immigrants Today

In 1991 more than 1.8 million legal immigrants came to the United States. The number broke the old record for most immigrants in a year—almost 1.3 million—set in 1907. Some of the 1991 immigrants had actually entered the country earlier, illegally. As part of the 1986 *amnesty* (pardon) programs, they became legal immigrants in 1991 and were counted that year. In 1996 the number of legal immigrants was 915,000. From 1991 to 1996 more than 6.1 million people entered America, and the country was on a pace to break the previous record for most immigrants in one decade. The previous record, about 8.7 million, was set from 1901 to 1910.

According to the U.S. Census Bureau, in 1996 America had about 24 million foreign-born residents. They made up about nine percent of the country's total population of 264 million. Almost 8 million of the immigrants were *naturalized* citizens—they had taken the official oath of U.S. citizenship. There were 16.6 million whites, about 2 million blacks, 5.6 million Asians, and just under 1 million Native Americans. Slightly more than 10 million immigrants lived in the West. The Midwest had the fewest foreign-born residents, with just 2.5 million.

The Immigration and Naturalization Service (INS) estimates that about 275,000 illegal immigrants enter the country each year. Mexico sends an average of 154,000 per year. Other countries of origin for illegal immigrants include Guatemala, El Salvador, and Canada. In 1996 the INS reported turning back more than 1.6 million

people who wanted to enter the United States, but the figure included criminals as well as undocumented aliens. Also, some illegal immigrants are caught entering the country and turned back, only to try again at a later time and be caught again.

Disaster in New York

Although Americans often stereotype illegal immigrants as poor Mexicans sneaking across the border, immigrants from all over the world try to enter the United States illegally. Many pay a high price to come. In 1993 the *Golden Venture* incident showed just how high the cost could be.

An old freighter named the *Golden Venture* sailed from Thailand carrying almost 300 illegal Chinese immigrants. The people had paid up to $35,000 each in return for safe, undetected entry into the United States. When the ship reached New York Harbor, however, trouble began. A smaller boat was supposed to meet the *Golden Venture* to bring the passengers ashore. When that boat never arrived, the smugglers on the ship decided to come as close to the shore as possible, then release the immigrants.

Sailing in the dark, the *Golden Venture* hit a sandbar, and in the following chaos ten passengers died. One rescuer described the scene: "They were jumping off, climbing down the ladders, trying to swim, but the current kept pulling them toward the jetties.... By the time they got to shore, they couldn't even stand."

U.S. officials brought 276 people ashore—just some of the thousands of Chinese who tried to enter America illegally during the 1990s. Most of the passengers of the *Golden Venture* were detained as illegal immigrants. The last of them was released from custody in 1997.

Today's immigrants, like many of the "new" immigrants of the early 20th century, are drawn to the nation's cities. In New York City about 50 percent of the population is made up of the foreign born and their children. Los Angeles, Chicago, and the cities of Texas and Florida also attract large numbers of immigrants. The immigrants are entering the country's large cities as more native-born Americans are

Countries of Origin

Below are the ten countries that supplied the most immigrants to the United States in 1996:

Country	Number
Mexico	163,572
Philippines	55,876
India	44,859
Vietnam	42,067
China	41,728
Dominican Republic	39,604
Cuba	26,466
Ukraine	21,079
Russia	19,668
Jamaica	19,089

Below are the ten countries that supplied the most immigrants to the United States between 1981 and 1996:

Country	Number
Mexico	3,304,682
Philippines	843,741
Vietnam	719,239
China	539,267
Dominican Republic	509,902
India	498,309
Korea	453,018
El Salvador	362,225
Jamaica	323,625
Cuba	254,193

SOURCE: U.S. Immigration and Naturalization Service

moving out to smaller cities and the suburbs.

■ Still "Out of Many, One"

Before the United States was officially created, an English immigrant saw the role America played for the world. In his essay, *Common Sense* (1776), Thomas Paine wrote, "… This new world hath been the asylum for the persecuted lovers of liberty from *every part* of Europe." Since then the rest of the world's continents have also sent immigrants seeking liberty.

Today, as in the past, many Americans seem to have mixed feelings about immigration. Most are proud of their own ethnic immigrant roots, and they want to think the United States still welcomes new arrivals seeking liberty. Yet many people feel some unease about the surge of immigration that began in 1965. The two attitudes toward immigrants that have pervaded throughout American history still exist. On the one hand America is a refuge for the immigrant. The country does provide liberty and willingly takes the immigrants' labor. On the other hand *nativism* (anti-immigrant feelings) and racism create fear of certain immigrants and the cultures they bring. Economic concerns also influence the debate on whether to accept or reject immigrants.

In 1997 the Knight-Ridder newspaper chain sponsored a poll on immigration. Native-born Americans and immigrants who arrived before 1980 were asked their attitudes toward immigration. Forty-five percent said it helped the country, 42 percent said it hurt the country, and the rest had mixed feelings or no opinion. That poll showed a marked change from one taken four years earlier, when 60 percent said immigration had a bad effect on America.

America still wants to believe its motto, *E pluribus unum,* "Out of many, one." Even if it cannot—or should not—be a melting pot, the country can unify its citizens around common goals and beliefs. In his 1998 State of the Union speech President Bill Clinton reflected that idea, stating, "We must work together, learn together, live together, and serve together…. Americans of all backgrounds can hammer out a common identity…. With shared values, honest communication and citizen service, we can unite a diverse people in freedom and mutual respect. We are many. We must be one."

FURTHER READING

Anderson, Kelly. *Immigration*. San Diego: Lucent Books, 1993.

Ashabranner, Brent K. Photos by Jennifer Ashabranner. *Still a Nation of Immigrants*. New York: Cobblehill, 1993.

Backer, Karen. *Immigration: Then & Now*. New York: Scholastic, 1997.

Coan, Peter M. *Ellis Island Interviews: In Their Own Words*. New York: Facts on File.

Collier, C., and J. L. Collier. *American Immigrants, 1840–1900*. Tarrytown, NY: Marshall Cavendish, 1999.

Cozic, Charles. *Illegal Immigration*. San Diego: Greenhaven Press, 1996.

Davies, Wendy. *Closing the Borders*. Austin, TX: Raintree Steck-Vaughn Publishers, 1995.

Freedman, Russell. *Immigrant Kids*. New York: Puffin, 1995.

Hadden, Gerald. *Teenage Refugees from Guatemala Speak Out*. New York: The Rosen Publishing Group, 1997.

Horrell, Sarah. *The History of Emigration from Eastern Europe* (Origins). Danbury: Franklin Watts, 1998.

Jacobs, Nancy R., Mark A. Siegel, and Alison Laudes, eds. *Immigration: Looking for a New Home*. Wylie, TX: Information Plus, 1997.

Jacobs, William Jay. *Ellis Island: New Hope in a New Land*. New York: Atheneum, 1990.

Kawaguchi, Gary, and Miriam Sagan. *Tracing Our Japanese Roots*. Santa Fe: John Muir Publications, 1994.

Kroll, Steven. Illus. by Karen Ritz. *Ellis Island: Doorway to Freedom*. New York: Holiday House, 1995.

Kurelek, William, and Margaret Engelhart. *They Sought a New World: The Story of European Immigration to North America*. Plattsburgh, NY: Tundra Books, 1988.

Ladybird Staff. *Migrations*. New York: Penguin USA, 1997.

Lawlor, Veronica. *I Was Dreaming to Come to America: Memories from the Ellis Island Oral History Project*. New York: Viking Children's Books, 1995.

Leder, Jane M. *The Russian Jewish Experience*. Minneapolis: The Lerner Publishing Group, 1996.

Lee, Kathleen. *Tracing Our Italian Roots* (American Origins). Santa Fe: John Muir Publications, 1993.

Levine, Ellen. Illus. by Wayne Parmenter. *If Your Name Was Changed at Ellis Island*. Scholastic Trade, 1994.

Levine, Herbert M. *Immigration*. Austin, TX: Raintree Steck-Vaughn Publishers, 1998.

Levinson, David, and Melvin Ember, eds. *American Immigrant Cultures: Builders of a Nation*. Vols. I & II. Indianapolis: MacMillan Publishing, 1997.

Morrow, Robert. *Immigration: Blessing or Burden?* Minneapolis: The Lerner Publishing Group, 1997.

Moscinski, Sharon. *Tracing Our Irish Roots* (American Origins). Santa Fe: John Muir Publications, 1993.

Prior, Katherine. *The History of Emigration from Italy* (Origins). Danbury: Franklin Watts, 1998.

Reef, Catherine. *Ellis Island* (Places in American History). Dillon Press, 1991.

Rollyson, Carl. *Teenage Refugees from Eastern Europe Speak Out*. New York: The Rosen Publishing Group, 1997.

Sandler, Martin W., and James Billington. *Immigrants* (A Library of Congress Book). New York: HaperCollins Juvenile Books, 1995.

Schapper, Ladena. *Teenage Refugees from Ethiopia Speak Out*. New York: The Rosen Publishing Group, 1997.

Stein, Richard Conrad. *Ellis Island* (Cornerstones of Freedom). Danbury: Children's Press, 1994.

Steoff, Rebecca, and Ronald Takaki. *Spacious Dreams: The First Wave of Asian Immigration* (The Asian American Experience). Broomall, PA: Chelsea House, 1994.

Strom, Yale. *Quilted Landscapes: Immigrant Youth in the United States*. Simon & Schuster, 1996.

Takaki, Ronald. *Ethnic Islands: The Emergence of Urban Chinese America* (The Asian American Experience). Broomall, PA: Chelsea House, 1994.

Tanner, Helen Hornbeck, Janice Reiff, and John H. Long, eds. *The Settling of North America: The Atlas of the Great Migrations into North America from the Ice Age to the Present*. Indianapolis: MacMillan Publishing, 1996.

Twagilimana, Aimable. *Teenage Refugees from Rwanda Speak Out*. New York: The Rosen Publishing Group, 1997.

Viswanath, Rupa. *Teenage Refugees from India Speak Out*. New York: The Rosen Publishing Group, 1997.

SET INDEX

numbers of, **7**:3-4, 5, 6, 8, 9
"picture brides", **7**:4
prejudice against, **7**:4, 7-10
religion, **7**:5, 6, 10
relocation camps (World War II), **7**:8-9
schools, **7**:7
sojourners, **7**:4
war brides, **7**:5
in World War II, **7**:8-9
Jewish history, **7**:12-16
Jewish immigrants
Ashkenazic, **7**:13-14, 17, 23-24
"brain drain", **7**:29
in colonial times, **7**:16-17
employment, **7**:18-19, 20, 29
from Eastern Europe and Russia, **7**:19-20, 24-25
from Europe, **7**:14-15
famous, **7**:25, 28, 29-31
from Germany, **7**:17-19, 24
locations settled in, **7**:18, 20
numbers of, **7**:17, 19-20, 22
in politics, **8**:88-89
prejudice against, **1**:46-47; **7**:25-28
prejudice among selves, **7**:24-25
Sephardic, **7**:13-14, 16-17, 18, 23-24
from Soviet Union, **7**:22; **9**:80, 83, 85, 86
from Turkey, **10**:69
during World War II, **7**:21-22, 25
Zionism, **7**:15-16, 25
Johnson-Reed Act. *See* Immigration law, Immigration Act of 1924
Jordanians. *See* Arabs
Journey to America, **3**:47-49; **6**:34, 64-65; **8**:34-35; **9**:3-4; **10**:65-69

K

Kampucheans (Cambodians). *See* Southeast Asians
Korea, history of, **7**:34-35
Korean immigrants
churches, **7**:37
employment, **7**:37
in Hawaii, **7**:36
locations settled in, **7**:37
numbers of, **7**:37
"picture brides", **7**:36
refugees, **7**:36
war brides, **7**:36
Kurdish immigrants
locations settled in, **7**:39
numbers of, **7**:39
refugees, **7**:39
Kurds, history of, **7**:38-39

L

Language issues, **7**:40-46
Laotians. *See* Southeast Asians
Latvia, history of, **7**:46-47
Latvian immigrants
churches, **7**:48
employment, **7**:47
locations settled in, **7**:47
music, **7**:48
numbers of, **7**:46

Lazarus, Emma, **2**:90; **7**:65; **10**:48-49
Leadership, **7**:50-57
Lebanese. *See* Arabs
Literacy, **5**:14; **7**:57-60
Literature, **7**:60-79. *See also* Arts
How the Other Half Lives. See Riis, Jacob
Maggie: A Girl of the Streets. See Crane, Stephen
The Promised Land. See Antin, Mary
slavery, **7**:62-63, 73-76
stereotypes, immigrant, **7**:61-62
The Uprooted. See Handlin, Oscar
Lithuania, history of, **7**:79-80
Lithuaniam immigrants
employment, **7**:81-82
ethnic centers, **7**:82
famous, **4**:22
and homeland independence, **7**:81, 82
locations settled in, **7**:81
mutual aid societies, **7**:82
numbers of, **7**:79
relations with Polish immigrants, **7**:82
saloons, **7**:82
Living conditions, illegal immigrants, **6**:12
Living conditions, immigrants, **5**:27-29; **6**:21; **7**:85-92; **10**:31-33
Africans, **3**:5, 13
Albanians, **3**:14
Basques, **3**:52
Finns, **5**:40
Gypsies, **5**:83
Haitians, **5**:87-88
Hungarians, **6**:67-68
Irish, **6**:67-68
Italians, **6**:86
Mexicans, **8**:9
Norwegians, **8**:35-36
Poles, **8**:70-71
Swedes, **10**:53
in time periods
in colonial times, **7**:85
in mid-1800s, **7**:86-87
in late 1800s, **7**:87-89
in early 1900s, **7**:87-89
in mid-1900s, **7**:89-91
in late 1900s, **7**:89-91
Locations settled in by immigrants, **9**:3.
See also Immigrants, migration within America; Population, immigrant, settlement patterns
Albanians, **3**:14
Armenians, **3**:24
Australians, **3**:40
Austrians, **3**:41
Basques, **3**:51-52, 53
Bosnians, **3**:56
Bulgarians, **3**:58
Chinese, **3**:88, 89
Croats, **4**:12-13
Cubans, **4**:17, 18
Czechs, **4**:43, 44, 45, 46
Danes, **4**:53, 56
Dutch, **1**:11-12; **4**:61-63
English, **5**:5-7
Estonians, **5**:21

Text printed on 70# Courtland matte, with Birch embossed endsheets
Printer: World Color Book Services, Taunton, MA.

Covers designed by Smart Graphics, East Haddam, CT; printed on 80# C1S
post-embossed. Cover printer: Mid-City Lithographers, Lake Forest, IL.